POWER, POISE,
AND PRESENCE

POWER, POISE, AND PRESENCE

A NEW APPROACH
TO AUTHENTIC LEADERSHIP

LIZETTE WARNER, PHD

NEW DEGREE PRESS

POWER, POISE, AND PRESENCE
A New Approach to Authentic Leadership

ISBN	979-8-88926-619-8	*Paperback*
	979-8-88926-621-1	*Hardcover*
	979-8-88926-620-4	*Ebook*

Dedication

To Shawn, Raph, and Peach, who've been on this
Power, Poise, and Presence journey with me.

To Mom and Dad, who taught me more than I ever learned in school.

Contents

———

Introduction

The first time I saw what I thought was power was when an older girl lit the papers she told me to hold while pointing to where I should stand in her basement, doing the same to her little sister. Two minutes later, she was stamping out the flames of the mattress on fire, and my four-year-old sensibilities woke up, urging me to get my dad next door. He pulled the girls out of the basement, also dragging out the burning mattress saving the house and preventing the neighborhood from going up in flames.

I realized power wasn't in someone telling me what and how to do things. My dad's fire-burned hands embodied power. He willingly risked his life and our livelihood. I learned presence was having clarity of purpose without doubting or second-guessing myself. Decades later, I forgot these lessons.

My husband lost his job two years before I anticipated graduating with my PhD. Our two kids, our house, the car we drove, and the food we ate depended on him working. He lost his job. I lost my confidence. I thought, *quit school, get a job,* or *move back home.* I didn't expect to remember my father's charred and bandaged hands, reminding me that my parents and our family somehow survived when my dad couldn't work. My perfect poise was born, and I emerged able to stay in discomfort and uncertainty to complete my PhD studies.

This book is the story of your power, poise, and presence. Trust me; you won't have to run from a burning house or lose your job to find it.

I wrote this book for my clients, women juggling multiple priorities and looking for level ground, men wondering what to do with their discomfort, and for the leaders this world needs.

This book, born of the fire sending me running for help, ignites this story of your authentic leadership, awaiting your discovery.

What I found working with women, whether she held a VP, director, project manager, CFO, CMO, or entrepreneur role, was that they were facing real and similar struggles:

- Feeling they had little power to act in their roles.
- Losing their confidence or doubting themselves.
- Criticizing themselves or feeling ashamed if they didn't have all the answers.
- Being uncomfortable with risk, staying too long in a role they had long outgrown.

It wasn't only women struggling. My male clients were also waging their battles.

- Taking on other's work and correcting it until it was right.
- Not feeling they had the power to change anything.
- Feeling stuck.
- Being unsure how to show up because they didn't have good leadership models.
- Hiding their discomfort from everyone or blowing up like Vesuvius for others to watch in horror.

Impostor syndrome strikes anyone, resulting in an eruption for all to see or paralysis, similar to being trapped inside a burning house, running out of options.

I needed an intentional approach beyond the story of a fire and a lost job to help others. I wanted to fix a seemingly pervasive, unyielding, and all-consuming problem people in my neighborhood were facing, being powerful when feeling powerless, being poised in uncertainty, and being present when in doubt. In a word, leadership.

Like the little girl running for help, I equipped myself with everything I needed. I studied trends, observed leaders' actions in private and public, researched various published studies, investigated the latest neuroscience findings, asked curious questions, and reflected on my conversations and outcomes with my clients. What resulted left its mark on me, similar to my father's hands from his actions. I poured myself, wisdom, sensations, emotions, and observations into this book. What began with articles, workshops, and events aimed at helping women advance in leadership evolved into a story of leadership presence for everyone. Only you can describe your authentic leadership. It is for you to discover.

Reflecting on my experiences from the fiery and fateful day in the basement uncovered sensations I had ignored: my breathing, heartbeat, posture, and other sensations I embodied in experiencing what I thought was power. Someone telling me what to do and how to do it was powerlessness. People often lament that they don't have the power to be change agents. My memory of a four-year-old who almost burned down a building and moved people twice her age out of her path rejects this assumption.

The realization of my power led me to get help. For all outward appearances, nothing changed. Standing in the basement, seemingly powerless, surrounded by fire, being told what to do, I knew everything was different. Time stopped. I planned all my next steps. Decades later, I remember the color and smell of the lawn, the deliberately focused path I traveled, and the fear I caused in anyone daring to get in my way. Yes, even as a four-year-old, I was a powerhouse.

As I grew older and wiser, the appreciation for both sides of power led me to try new techniques with people struggling with their expression of power. The methods I used revealed something my clients had never known they always knew. Together we found a simple way to allow them to have transformational insights and begin to do things differently from anything they had ever seen modeled by anyone else.

Gravitas describes leaders with executive presence. I find the literal definition for gravitas, *Je ne sais quoi*, meaning I don't know, useless. I ditched gravitas in favor of something clear and challenging to embody—poise.

Poise is being calm and balanced during uncertainty or volatility. I ran from the basement to tell an uncomfortable truth with poise. Poise was my father's composure in getting up and, with swift action, attending to the emergency I created. Reflecting on my poise and working with people to uncover theirs, we found specific patterns, attributes, characteristics, or markers for their poise, helping them pinpoint when they changed from not poised to poised. The same potatoes create mashed potatoes or scalloped potatoes. Each recipe is different. It is the same for power, poise, and presence. I was helping people unearth their unique biological markers signaling when they were well poised, allowing these same people to use these markers like a recipe to create their unique power, poise, or presence moments.

Presence is the aura radiating your state of being. Presence is rooted in confidence. In my experience, you can be present (little p) in any situation. If you want to exude Presence (capital P), you can't do it without confidence. These three—power, poise, and presence form the first stage of uncovering the heart of your authentic leadership.

When I helped people find their authentic leadership zone, they discovered something they never knew always existed within themselves and, once discovered, changed nothing and everything. I helped people uncover their biomarkers for power, poise, and presence. They told me how they used these biomarkers in their daily life, how power helped them rescue situations, how presence allowed them to land new jobs, and how poise uncovered the right thing to do when uncertain—and I wrote it all down in this book. They related how draining it was for them when operating outside their power, poise, and presence zone. I wrote everything they and I experienced in this book, hoping I could help others. The techniques I use and the findings I share will help guide you along your path to uncovering your power, poise, and presence.

Congratulations on your brave new future.

CHAPTER ONE

Why Power, Poise, and Presence

———

Growth is painful. Change is painful. But nothing is as painful as staying stuck somewhere you don't belong.

—MANDY HALE

"I don't know why I can't advance. I'm watching men move ahead. I finished the Ivy League Leadership Program. I passed with flying colors! Why am I struggling? Why can't I make it work for me?" said Bev, the robotics manager working in the defense sector. She was the only woman in her department and one of few in her field. She felt isolated and alone.

Repetitive conversations similar to this one inspired me to help other Bevs. People longed for a deep experience to fuel their professional trajectories from dejected, passive, or angry observers to empowered, balanced, and confident titans.

Titans communicate with power. Titans have poise, and most of all, others feel a Titan's presence. Power, poise, and presence are not something *for* you but rather something *of you*, your fragrance. Your power, poise, and presence fragrances are unique. The principles and techniques in this book will help you discover your characteristic scent-producing principles allowing you to show up with authentic power, poise, and presence.

Leadership presence is essential for anyone seeking professional, personal, or career growth. Your actions and communications are critical for your success regardless of the stage of your career. According to the Center for Talent Innovation, leadership presence is a top indicator of future promotions. The number one reason decision-makers exclude people from top leadership roles is lacking *executive presence* (Hewitt 2013). Executive presence is a vague mixture of looking and acting the part. Having a leadership presence can't be merely an *act*. Being the part is different from acting the part.

The best actors don't act. They *become* their role. If you want to discover your inner power, poise, and presence, by adopting a one size fits all set of postures, breathing exercises, or mental conjuring, then my approach is not for you. Put the book down and move on to the set of leadership presence books already lining the shelves instructing you how to act the part. If you are ready to face the monster, or the mouse, within yourself, the one sucking away or tiptoeing beside your power, poise, or presence, or you are ready to transform your monster or mouse into the Titan, bringing you energy, lifting you, and bringing your soul in harmony—if you are ready to *be* the part—then please continue.

WOMEN NEED POWER, POISE, AND PRESENCE

For all the advances women have made, few make it to the top of the business world. As of 2021, over 8 percent of Fortune 500 companies were led by women CEOs, forty-one out of 500 (Connley 2021). Considering that women make up half of the workforce and are the primary earners in 40 percent of families, 8 percent is nowhere near closing the gap (Wang 2013). Sparking change at the top by mandating diversity targets fails to include women in the conversation (Burns 2021).

The C-level, or the C-suite, describes the high-ranking executives in an organization. While only 8 percent of women-led Fortune 500 companies in 2021, globally, 29 percent of women were in a senior leadership role. In the US, 31 percent were in senior leadership roles (L 2021). According to a McKinsey Report on women in the workplace, the data of men and women climbing the corporate ladder show men being far more successful in reaching the C-suite than women, with 70 percent of men compared to 30 percent of the women in senior leadership roles below the C-level.

Men and women had different journeys to the C-suite (Burns 2021). Despite women being half of the entry-level workforce, they failed to advance compared to the fast-tracked men. The outlook is worse for Black, Hispanic, and Asian women (LeanIn.Org 2022). This is nothing new. Marilyn Loden coined the phrase *glass ceiling* to acknowledge the invisible barriers women faced in the workforce over forty years ago (Caceres-Rodriguez 2013).

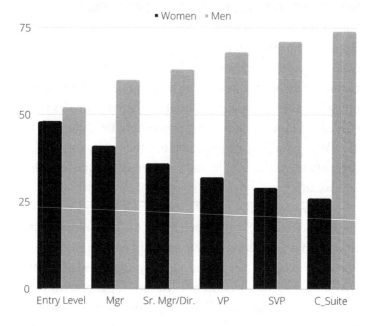

Figure 1. Role and gender corporate representation—compiled from data sourced from Women in the Workplace 2022, Leanin. org, and McKinsey 2021 (LeanIn.Org 2022).

Forty years later, few women successfully climbed the corporate ladder after entering the workforce. While the data from McKinsey showed the number of men and women entering the workplace were similar, 52 percent and 48 percent, respectively, both women of color and white women lost ground at each step up the corporate ladder compared to men of color and white men, 24 percent to 75 percent at the C-suite—the highest rung on the corporate ladder (Burns 2021; LeanIn.Org 2022). The data was both undeniable and deflating. The data dismayed me. Women were advancing into leadership roles at a depressing and slower pace than their male peers.

Exasperated women were sharing with me their struggles to advance in their careers. I witnessed the lack of actionable feedback they were getting from their leaders, understood their sense of feeling left out of crucial conversations, observed their lack of support, and witnessed the opportunities to widen their networks shrink. These conversations were similar regardless of the industry or their level in the organization. Surprisingly, my male clients complained of facing similar hurdles to their female peers. However, they handled it differently—and neither were handling their hurdles well.

The women verbalized their exasperation, leaned into frustration, and prepared to stomach their situation thinking there was little they could do because the risk was too great to leave their employer. Often, these women would explore leaving once convinced that leaving was the next step. Men, on the other hand, would lose their tempers, ball their fists, ready to punch a wall or risk the uncertainty of moving, many times leaving for another company or a different field.

While bias, prejudice against or in favor of a person or certain group, slows a women's leadership progression, laws and workplace equity measures attempt to correct bias discrimination. Correcting unconscious bias and stereotypes outside of conscious awareness is more complicated. Studies show that small gender biases lead to similar gender disparities observed in the McKinsey study. Mandating leadership or executive roles to get to gender equity leads to short-term gains in gender equity, only to return to the initial disparities within a few years, according to study results (Nordell 2021).

Aside from bias, arguments concerning motherhood pulling women away from career opportunities suggest that the lower levels of women in higher leadership roles are due to motherhood. However, various studies have shown that companies push women out of the workforce due to workplace inflexibilities, long working hours, lack of support for boundaries, or the high volume of work (Lim 2019; Salem 2022; McCarthy 2021). Conversely, women deciding to lead has shown merit in a study of emergency medicine leaders (Guptill 2018). Whatever the root cause: bias, feeling pushed or pulled, or deciding to lead or not, the fact remains that fewer women are rising into similar career levels compared to men and are, meanwhile, facing unique external and internal challenges.

POWER, POISE, AND PRESENCE FOR MEN?
The unique internal challenges are showing up powerful when feeling powerless, poised amid uncertainty, and being present with confidence when fear or doubt takes hold. Women aren't the only ones needing power, poise, and presence. Any method touting how to stand, how to project, who to be like, or whom to emulate belittles the truth. You need to stand, project, and be you. Men can fear others' perceptions of what or how they should be. They suit up with power, poise, and presence—someone else's.

Men may show confidence. Similar to the actor, they can act the role instead of becoming the part, knowing how to trigger the behavior and live with the discomfort. Outwardly, they may show confidence. Inwardly they wring their hands and build up stress. Eventually, stress may manifest in outbursts, burnout, or anger. If these outbursts are a chronic stress response, the long-term repercussions are cardiovascular disease, heart attacks, stroke, obesity, and more.

Mental stress over a lifetime may contribute to heart disease and cardiovascular episodes (Vaccarino 2021). A recent study shows that men undergoing multiple divorces are at an increased risk for heart disease (Johns Hopkins Medicine 2021). Men may display a strong show of emotion, anger, blow-ups, or blaming, all due to mishandling power, poise, and presence. Yes, men need power, poise, and presence too.

BENEFITS

Labeling the disparity of women at the top as a *woman's problem* is both a fallacy and truth. Lacking women in leadership roles is a challenge women face. The fallacy is that women aren't the only ones losing out. Entire organizations are suffering by not having women in leadership roles. Society demands equity, and equity pays. The most recent report from the International Labour Organization (ILO) highlights that having more women in decision-making positions can improve business profitability (Viveros 2019).

Gender diversity boosts economies. Accenture, a global professional service company, calculates that the GDP (global gross domestic product) would increase by up to $8 trillion by 2028 if we raised the innovation mindset by 10 percent in all countries (Shook 2021). Accenture proclaims that if "organizations want to thrive, they have to get equal." Corroborating

Accenture's claims, the Organisation for Economic Co-operation and Development estimates that reducing the labor force gender gap by 50 percent would lead to an additional GDP gain of 6 percent (OECD 2017).

Women are supporting their employees' well-being, leading to happier, less burned-out employees, thus reducing the attrition rate (Burns 2021). Happy employees are effective employees—productivity trended up to 62.8 percent. According to the ILO, higher productivity correlates to business profits, which are directly linked to gender diversity (Viveros 2019). Women increase the bottom line for the organization, and for organizations to benefit, studies suggest they need to reach a critical mass of women at the top (Viveros 2019; Shook 2019). The stakes are enormous.

Understanding the importance of a diverse workforce, including having women in top leadership roles, doesn't quell the struggle to retain women, advance them into leadership roles and keep them in those roles. Leadership quotas may help level the field at first. Without women believing they belong in those roles, having resiliency for what frustrates them, and bearing confidence in being their authentic best, women may continue to struggle or leave the workplace (Nordell 2021; Guptill 2018; LeanIn.org 2022).

The cost of an up-skill initiative for half the workforce is an expensive undertaking for any organization. However, the price of inaction is costlier. The Workforce Institute estimates that an employee's replacement costs the company a conservative 30 percent of an employee's salary (Mahan 2020).

REAL REASON

What is the real reason behind women not advancing in their careers similar to their male counterparts? Women tend to stay out of the spotlight and promote others' work instead of their own, perhaps, partly because women engaging in self-promotion can suffer backlash or reprisals (Rudman 1998; Moss-Racusin 2010). Women tend to self-promote less often or may undervalue their accomplishments compared to their male counterparts (Moss-Racusin 2010; Exley 2022).

A recent ILO study found that women were over-represented in support management functions: HR, facilities, and administration. Men were over-represented in strategic management functions: risk, visioning, planning, and financial analysis (Viveros 2019).

Strategic management roles serve as the springboard to CEO and board-level positions. According to the ILO, when women receive promotions into leadership roles, they promote into supportive management roles, not strategic ones. Medical fields show women are assistants and associate deans working on education, diversity, and faculty affairs and rarely in influential and strategic clinical or research roles (Lautenberger 2020). However, a few women are advancing into strategic leadership roles.

The successful women in emergency medicine from earlier have more than the casual intention to lead in strategic roles, making strategic roles a life goal (Guptill 2018). Beyond setting the intention to lead, these successful leaders sought support personnel: mentors, sponsors, and coaches. These successful leaders intended their work and life to support their leadership aims. Thus, they planned according to their intentions. Converse to popular opinion, women have mastered using time to support work and home life (Vanderkam 2017).

Studying women advancing into strategic leadership roles may shed light on their peers struggling to follow their advancing examples. Beyond the intentionality of deciding to lead observed in emergency medicine leaders, a study of medical trainees reveals insights from the other end of the leadership spectrum (Guptill 2018).

Researchers observed male and female medical fellows simulating an emergency cardiopulmonary rescue in male or female-led, single-gendered, and mixed-gendered teams where, unbeknownst to participants, researchers gauged their leadership potential. When women were in the lead, regardless of the team composition, there was more chaos, a lack of clear guidance, and a failure to follow through on instructions (Amacher 2017). The lack of leader confidence, presence, assertiveness, and poise led to weaker team performance in the simulation. Peers and supervisors deemed female leads as poor leaders (Dayal 2016). The observation of her performance being poor also led to her peers judging her as not being leadership material. We need greater progress earlier in the leadership pipeline for all (Lautenberger 2020).

When coaching men or women, I often hear, "I'm not showing up the way I know I should," or, "I'm trying to be what I think is expected or acceptable, and it doesn't feel right," and doubt takes hold. If they are anything similar to my male clients, the male leaders from the medical study probably didn't have any stronger poise or confidence than their female counterparts. My male clients tend not to let doubt, lack of confidence, or discomfort stop them from acting in the moment. Both men and women are uncomfortable. The difference is that women are perhaps letting discomfort disrupt their *ability* to act, while men are letting discomfort control *how* they act.

While my male clients might say they don't "feel comfortable," they'll go on to show up confident, bark orders, or risk acting a certain way. My female clients might say they "neither feel nor *act* confident nor the way they want." In fact, my female clients will lose all remaining confidence when even small doubts arise.

My male clients want to feel comfortable with the discomfort of not feeling confident. The discomfort leads them to question what outside of themselves is off. My female clients want to figure out what is *wrong* with them and how to act with confidence, even if they don't necessarily feel it. My female clients, similar to Audrey, someone you'll meet later, will "want to learn how not to crumble."

Often, people emulate the behavior they see in others achieving their goals. Imagine me trying to jump and twirl and almost breaking my neck, thinking I could be the next Simone Biles. The truth is I don't have her skill, talent, or, most importantly, her years of training. When I think I can be her by mimicking what she does, I am being delusional. Sure, if I practice, I can then learn—if I want to dedicate all my life toward those skills similar to how Simone has, or I could rather appreciate gymnastics from afar. I chose the latter. Pretty quick, if I'm honest.

If a strong leader is loud and boisterous and is all you've ever known, then you might also try being loud and boisterous. I'm not saying you are delusional. I would invite you to think broader. If you are not, by nature, wired for loud and boisterous behavior and insist on putting this behavior into practice, you might feel sore and worn out. I was sore, dizzy, and worn out in my twirling escapades. You may come across disingenuous or phony because being loud and boisterous isn't in your nature.

In my twirling escapades, I expended a ton of energy. By the end of a few twirls, I was exhausted, aside from being bruised. If you are doing something outside your natural or built-up skillset, you may be uncomfortable, use up loads of energy and fail to demonstrate your desired outcome. While I was trying to twirl and bounce, similar to Simone, my appendages wouldn't move and rotate at odd angles. My escapades battered, bruised, and exhausted me. I easily communicated with my performance and emotions. "Lizette is not a gymnast, nor will she ever be."

Our behaviors and emotions communicate similarly to words or gestures to those near us. Mine did. Behavior study experiments have suggested that others' emotions affect us at an incredible pace. We pick up on others' emotions and infect others with our emotions (Reis 2009). Indeed, this emotional contagion may explain the peer perception patterns from the medical resident studies.

EMOTIONAL CONTAGION AND EMBODIED EXPERIENCES

Emotions or sensations are not accidental. Discomfort, for example, has a physical manifestation, an experience, telling a vibrant story. We often ignore the story or focus on the uncomfortable experience alone. I might relive a discomfort from my life on a constant loop, ruminating on it. In the case of the medical trainees in leadership roles, they may have ignored the embodied wisdom their discomfort communicated to them. Those sensations may have been trying to say, "this behavior doesn't fit you." I don't take my husband's or my mom's medication because doctors prescribe it for them. When uncomfortable sensations rise up, they may be similar to the medication label, telling you, "not your meds."

External forces aren't responsible for people being poor leaders. We benefit from honoring and listening to the emotions and sensations we and others experience.

In a workshop I conducted, someone asked, "How can I avoid the fear of missing out that pushes me to attend all these meetings?"

How I answered isn't important now. You'll find out in a later chapter. What is important is, after the workshop, one attendee commented in private, "Your impactful and insightful reply was counteracted" by my final response of, "I don't know if that's helpful for you?" communicating to the audience that I wasn't confident in my response.

As a coach, I don't want to lead my clients in distinct directions or tell them what to do. I thought that with my reply,

I was granting attendees the ability to choose what to do with the knowledge I shared, at the price of suggesting I lacked confidence. I changed my language to communicate, "I am confident in my message," while allowing attendees the freedom to use the information I shared. I replaced my final question with this one: "What do you want to do with this knowledge?"

While I can't control how others perceive me, I can change what I do, say, act, and the emotions I embody, influencing their perceptions. I can doubt myself and ruminate on what I should have done, or I can choose to act with the knowledge I gained and move forward. When we doubt, it is possible we are influencing others with our contagious emotions, affecting their emotions and perceptions, and communicating poor leadership potential.

Rather than ignore, ruminate, or get stuck with what you experience, I invite you to explore your power, poise, and presence. We will explore your sensations, emotions, knowledge, and experiences to uncover how to use the wisdom in these pages uncovering new insights for you.

CHAPTER TWO

Biomarkers

———

Not I nor anyone else can travel that road for you. You must travel it by yourself. It is not far. It is within reach.

—WALT WHITMAN

A ONE-WAY STREET

After you eat a meal, your blood glucose levels rise, and cells in your pancreas secrete insulin, a hormone causing your body to absorb the glucose circulating in your blood, returning your glucose levels to normal. Insulin-compromised patients' bodies can't produce enough insulin, or the insulin is ineffective. Insulin-compromised patients track their blood glucose with a glucose meter to make appropriate interventions to keep their glucose levels in a normal range to avoid long-term complications.

Glucose is a biomarker of diabetes. The National Institute of Health says a biomarker is a characteristic objectively measured and evaluated, an indicator of normal biological processes, pathogenic processes, or pharmacologic responses to a therapeutic intervention. In nonspecialists' terms, biomarkers are measurable substances pointing to disease or health (NIH 2021).

According to the Federal Drug Administration (FDA), there are four types of biomarkers: molecular, histologic, radiographic, and physiologic (United States Food and Drug Administration 2021). The concept of biomarkers serves us in examining your characteristics, power, poise, and presence, similar to the blood glucose meter results.

A blood glucose meter measures blood glucose, and it's a one-way street, meaning the meter will give you a value for glucose in your blood and doesn't impact the source, your blood, your body, or the way your body processes glucose.

What if I told you the results from the glucose meter could be used to change disease into health in your body with nothing more than the biomarker? You'd call me delusional. Your blood glucose level measured from your glucose meter can't change the insulin released in your body or your insulin's effectiveness. Your glucose measure is at the end of a one-way street. The types of biomarkers we use in this book are a two-way street.

HOW WE USE BIOMARKERS
We go through life feeding the *meter*, resulting in characteristics, for example, power or powerlessness emerging. Take this example. After a presentation, you think to yourself, "I've done a good job," because "People are giving me good

feedback," and "My boss looks happy with me." Therefore I feel empowered or proud.

When we break this down, here is an example of what might be happening. Into our biomarker meter goes "feel good about the work," "hearing good feedback," "seeing a happy boss," and out pops the reading *empowered* or *proud* or whatever it conjures up for you.

Feeling, hearing, and seeing are all physiological biomarkers. These physiological biomarkers exist along a measurable spectrum. I can feel a little to a lot. I can hear or see fuzzy to clear. Even if I don't experience a spectrum of possibilities, the spectrum exists. The reading popping out of the meter is the characteristic you label power, poise, presence, or something else.

Many of us live a life of servitude to the meter and experience the element reported out, rarely realizing the biomarker we feed into the meter is under our control. The analogy would be changing your insulin level or your insulin's effectiveness, thus changing the glucose circulating in your blood and the meter's results.

Someone may argue, "change the meter," ensuring that regardless of what biomarkers you present, your confidence emerges, for example. *You* are the meter. Changing the meter may be beyond your control. Changing your biomarkers are in your control. You control your input biomarkers.

The biomarkers you feed your meter are necessary components leading to your desired characteristics. This will give you a baseline to understand your meter. I will teach you how to discover your biomarkers by traveling in both directions on your two-way street, successfully feeding the meter for your desired results. Once you have this knowledge, you can provide the meter with the biomarkers you identify to show up the way you want.

THE NEUROSCIENCE BEHIND BIOMARKERS

You can consider your feelings, bodily movements, sensations, emotions, and memories, all biomarkers. Memories are the most complicated because they evoke strong feelings, movements, sensations, emotions, and the memory's characteristics. Recall a powerful memory and see what sensations and characteristics rise for you.

Weeks after my brother died of pancreatic cancer, I remember breaking down in tears when I heard the lawnmower hum and smelled freshly mowed grass. I remember the room I was standing in when the smell of fresh-cut grass hit me, reminding me of the landscape business he would never operate again. Those sensations reminded me of our summers in Chicago, the quiet strength I found in our relationship, and the peace he found. The memory carves itself into my body, sensations, emotions, smells, and sounds. Whenever I bring this memory up, I experience him and the peace flowing from years of shared experiences. Memories are full of biomarkers.

Think of biomarkers akin to ingredients in your kitchen, memories full of fragrance and flavor in the spice rack, dry goods of all shapes and sizes in the pantry, leafy vegetables of various textures, and milk and juices of different heaviness and colors in the refrigerator. We are awash with biomarkers.

Aromas emerge from the kitchen at any given moment. We may realize the aromas when cooking, and not at other times. What scent do you smell at this moment? All day long, we breathe, inhale and smell, unaware of the things we smell. While you may be unaware of all the scents, sensations, movements, feelings, emotions, sights, sounds, and temperatures you experience, your brain absorbs and processes all these. The brain uses all those extended spaces and biomarkers for cognitive thinking inputs. Thinking happens from the extended spaces your brain accesses (Paul 2021). Our work together will bring those symbolic spaces into your control, allowing you to mobilize your biomarkers and assemble your power, poise, and presence.

The characteristic emerging from my memory of my brother is one of peace. A recipe can form from characteristics, and your biomarkers are the ingredients. When I want to tap into my peace, I think of prayer. I am never alone in prayer. My peace is expansive. My peace smells similar to the healthy oils released from freshly cut grass. I see sunlight softened and layered through sheer curtains, allowing me to taste light, airy sweetness. My breath is soft and smooth. My mind is clear, and my thoughts are silent. If I were to write a recipe for my peace, it would read:

LIZETTE'S PEACE
1. Bring to mind prayer.
2. Imagine you are in good company.

3. Think expansiveness.
4. Add the smell of fresh-cut grass.
5. Layer in sunlight, soft and airy.
6. Taste sweetness.
7. Include soft and smooth breathing.
8. Clear your mind.
9. Silence your thoughts.

My peace recipe card contains my biomarkers. Your biomarkers for peace are probably different. You may trigger some of your peace through my peace recipe. Any one of my biomarkers may foul up your recipe for peace. If, however, my peace recipe works for you, I invite you to use it, modify it and make it yours. Your power, poise, and presence recipes are similar to this one.

WHAT ARE MY BIOMARKERS?

Knowing you have biomarkers can be exciting and lead you on a quest. In what direction should I travel? You may wonder, *What are my biomarkers, and what exactly makes something a biomarker?*

Biomarkers can be anything meaning something to you and a few things meaning nothing to you. Some biomarkers can be scents of my fresh-cut grass from earlier or sensations of expansiveness or thoughts of a clear mind, your breathing, or certain emotions. These biomarkers may make sense to you because when you think about an experience or a memory, these sensations may come to mind without much thinking. They arise from your senses, and you are conscious of them.

Other biomarker types are nonsensical. Even if I recall my peace from earlier, I didn't consider where it emerged—my heart, since you are wondering. We don't think about sensation saying, "Hmm, where might the center be?" Location can be an important marker. I rarely find the scissors in our kitchen because someone moved them from the drawer. Knowing the scissors have a home shows me where to look. A location is an important marker to discovering where a characteristic calls home.

NONSENSICAL BIOMARKERS

Aside from location, other nonsensical biomarkers attached to a characteristic can be:

- A color. Different characteristics may have a color for you.
- A name. Naming a collection of biomarkers may give the collection a home.
- A metaphor. A collection of biomarkers may be sparks of fire for you.
- Motion. From rigid or stillness to frenzied, activity may be present for you. Stillness was present for my peace.

When we work to identify your power, poise, and presence, we will work through both sense biomarkers and nonsensical biomarkers.

Biomarkers give you a wealth of resources, both internal and external. You may be wondering what meaning is behind: when my mind is spinning with thoughts, or my mind is calm, or when I feel my stomach soften, or when my shoulders relax, or when I find I'm breathing slowly? Biomarkers come together similarly to ingredients for a recipe. Any chef working to create a new signature recipe knows her ingredients, their look, taste, and feel, and how to find them. This is the first step toward revealing your signature power, poise, and presence biomarkers.

DISCOVERING YOUR BIOMARKERS

A biomarker tracker can help you know how often a biomarker is present and what is most associated with particular sensations. The first time I used a biomarker tracker was when I was trying to lose weight. In my family, a crying baby meant you gave the baby food. I was the gorged baby. I grew up eating a lot. I ate when I was hungry and when I wasn't hungry. When I got married to a husband whose family grew up through famine in Ireland, I learned that a crying baby meant there were many needs to check with the baby outside of providing food. It seemed bizarre to me since I learned to feed a crying baby to check if the baby was dirty, tired, bloated, or bored before I checked if they were hungry.

Our kids took lots of naps because my husband *is* the baby whisperer. He can put any baby to sleep. Only after our baby would wake up from a couple of naps and begin smacking their mouths would we feed our baby. Learning and seeing the signs of our babies' different communication patterns taught me to break my habit of hearing a crying baby and reaching for food. Exploring and breaking my food habits led me to track my hunger.

Tracking my hunger with a biomarker tracker taught me I didn't eat because of need. What was masquerading for hunger was a feeling of not being sure what to do.

Biomarker Tracker

Figure 1. Lizette's hunger biomarker tracker.

You might begin monitoring or observing your sensations. I had a goal when I was trying to figure out my hunger. You don't need a specific goal. Perhaps you want to:

- capture your mood throughout the day,
- identify how often you feel tired,
- notice when you are being kind to yourself,
- notice when you aren't being kind to yourself,
- track different body sensations, or
- track how often you laugh or smile during the day.

Biomarker Tracker

Biomarker	Tally

Figure 2. An empty biomarker tracker. Use the biomarker tracker to track different biomarkers. Notice different sensations throughout your day. You may even begin to discover a theme corresponding to when a biomarker is active for you.

You can use a tracker to jot sensations down without pointing fingers at yourself or anyone else. Track them. Be a scientist; notice without judging yourself. When you are noticing sensations, you are curious about what's happening and noticing you have biomarkers. Later you might get more sophisticated to notice when these biomarkers emerge or if there is a pattern. The more you track your biomarkers, the more biomarkers you will begin to see in you and others. Your body's biomarkers are the foundation for exploring your power, poise, and presence.

FEEDING YOUR BRAIN

If your body is an extension of your mind, the sensations and experiences you have with your body, processed by your brain, result in different characteristics: power, poise, presence, fear, etc. (Paul 2021). Take the case of the medical trainees from chapter 1. The trainees judged with poor leadership skills fostered chaos, demonstrated poor guidance to subordinates, gave unclear instructions, and lacked follow through. Something was happening within the individuals, leading to a poor demonstration of leadership.

What sensations were they experiencing? Research shows your brain will analyze your bodily sensations and prepare you to experience a characteristic, fear, for example (Paul 2021). I grew super curious to ask the trainees, "What might happen when the room is not chaotic and you are giving good guidance?" If you can feed your brain these sensations, drawing from a memory of recent success, your brain can process these biomarkers, manufacturing a different starting point.

Your starting point isn't an arbitrary location. You can impact your *desired* outcome by reframing your starting point with biomarkers. This is how you navigate traveling in the opposite direction on your two-way street. Your body speaks in sensations at all hours of the day, and your brain interprets these signals. We follow predetermined one-way paths, not knowing we have powerful control over defining the path using biomarkers (Paul 2021). We will not ignore the path in the work we do together. We will shine a light on your sensations in both directions. The cues your mind processes can reveal and generate your power, poise, and presence—the basis of your authentic leadership.

I'M NOT A FEELING PERSON

Everyone experiences sensations. Needing to go to the toilet is a sensation. Being hungry is a sensation. Each of us has varying degrees of awareness and abilities to discern these sensations. You may not be a *feeling* person. The feelings you do have come with sensations. The sensations you have for power, poise, and presence are distinct and unique to you. Understanding the component markers making up these characteristics will help you discover your singular way to emulate and embody your characteristics.

NEXT STEPS

You can apply my approach to anyone—colleagues, children, and youth. Those not prone to perceive emotions or sensations, or have a weak awareness muscle, may struggle with the following assessments. However, everybody with a pulse has physical and emotional sensations. If you notice sensations are absent, I suggest not digging too deep. If you don't feel, experience, or sense something, you should note its absence because an absence is an awareness of sensation too.

Use the biomarker tracker to pay attention to your sensations over the next few days.

POWER

POWER

CHAPTER THREE

Power

If knowledge is power, knowing what we don't know is wisdom.

—ADAM GRANT

Before delving into power, I want to introduce you to Ashley, a high achiever in marketing and media relations.

When I met Ashley, she told me, "I'm the go-to person on the team. If it's an impossible job, I'm the one finding a way to make it work. I'm part of the media relations team and the one meeting with executives coordinating our quarterly releases."

I was curious where this was leading when Ashley said, "My boss's boss, our vice president, asks me to do things outside my expertise and responsibilities in high-profile meetings where I can't say no. I'm marketing and media relations, and he wants me to fix the sales reporting from the field."

"I pull the data for our campaign to run the reports. When he points at those numbers and demands I answer why certain markets show data from nonrelevant products, I don't have an answer. I always have an answer, and I always know. Not with him. He shouted at me, saying I got it wrong and needed to fix it in front of my boss and other leaders. I feel ashamed and stupid. He's suggesting I don't know how to do my job. They pull the data from the market reports. He doesn't want to hear excuses. He's at the top of the organization, and he treats me this way in front of others, and I feel powerless."

"I have always outperformed my peers. I have always prepared and over-delivered anything asked of me. These quarterly Executive Team meetings with this jerk are ruining my life," said Ashley.

Ashley was at her wit's end with her leader's unreasonable demands and requests.

"Every few months, I must work on the campaign. I am working nights and weekends to prepare things for him. I review my deck and ensure I understand the data at least five layers into the data to have an answer when he decides to poke at what I've pulled together. I must prepare weeks ahead, gather deeper data, and understand the data. My husband asked me to put these campaigns on our family calendar. He takes the kids on outings, letting me have spreadsheets lining the kitchen table for the next campaign. Each quarter when the campaign needs to run, I meet the jerk. My life turns upside down. I spend these few weeks preparing for these quarterly grillings. I can't keep this up. I'm thinking of finding a new job. This team attracted me, and I love my coworkers and our work. This added campaign with a jerk is not what I thought I signed up to do."

The universe is replete with jerks. Finding your power can help you navigate the personalities in your universe. Ashley discovered her mighty self with a power assessment. I invite you to find your strong self with the following power assessment.

POWERLESSNESS AND POWER ASSESSMENT

Find a quiet space to ponder the following questions. If you turn off all distractions, it'll help you finish quicker. Be prepared to take a deep breath or five and show up for yourself to step into your power. Take your time completing this *entire* assessment section, powerlessness and power. We will first tap into the opposite of power and explore specific biomarkers.

If you can't complete both sections in a single sitting, then return to this later when you have time to complete both sections. Begin with powerlessness and continue onto the power section.

POWERLESSNESS

WHAT IS A CHALLENGE YOU ARE FACING NOW WHERE HAVING A POWERFUL PRESENCE WOULD BE HELPFUL FOR YOU?

We all face challenges, tough experiences, or moments when our actions are incongruent with our values. We can feel awkward or uncomfortable. We show up less powerfully than we would have preferred. What is the powerless moment you'd rewrite?

IN YOUR OWN WORDS, SUMMARIZE WHAT A LACK OF POWER IS TO YOU. BRING FORTH DETAILS.

When the moment arrives when you feel powerless, emotions can surface. Different bodily sensations can emerge. We conjure memories, and those memories may lead to more and more profound reactions. What are those reactions for you?

WHAT DOES YOUR IMAGINATION CONJURE WHEN YOU IMAGINE YOURSELF IN THE SPACE OF POWERLESSNESS? DRAW OR WRITE IT.

In the moment of being or feeling powerless, certain activities may arise. You may feel small, fidgety, and off-balanced, or you may picture yourself teetering near the cliff's edge. Visualizing your lack of power can help you recognize when you are approaching your powerless space.

WHAT COLOR IS POWERLESSNESS?

We are three-dimensional beings with a host of sensations that most creatures lack. Tapping into color may reveal additional insights into your lack of power. What color comes to mind associated with powerlessness, if any?

WHAT SHAPE DOES A LACK OF POWER HAVE?

Continuing the sensation journey, tap into the shape of powerlessness.

WHAT SENSATIONS DOES POWERLESSNESS PROVOKE?
Exploring when you lack power might signal other linked sensations. Becoming aware of powerlessness, what sensations are present?

DESCRIBE ONE OR TWO OF THOSE SENSATIONS MORE.
Sensations have associated actions and behaviors. If I'm weak or anxious, those sensations could cause me to feel off-balance and unsure of what to say next.

PICK THE MOST VITAL SENSATIONS ASSOCIATED WITH POWERLESSNESS. PLEASE TAKE A FEW MOMENTS TO CONSIDER ITS SOURCE OF ORIGIN. WHERE DOES IT ORIGINATE?
Sensations have homes. Powerlessness lives in a location with a GPS address. The GPS address can be outside, inside, or on your person. You are a creature with body, mind, and spirit. Where is the GPS location for your powerlessness?

SUMMARIZE YOUR POWERLESSNESS.
Having spent time getting to know your lack of power, you are well suited to identify its sensations, GPS location, behaviors, and characteristics. Having a summary of powerlessness tells you its home and neighborhood.

FROM THIS SPACE OF POWERLESSNESS, WHAT ARE YOUR MANNERISMS AND BEHAVIORS?
You act a certain way when you are in this home and neighborhood. You may experience fear, a tightness in your

shoulders, talk in a high-pitched voice or use any mannerisms appropriate for this home and community. What are yours?

POWER

This part of the journey will take us to a new neighborhood and a different home. Switching locations from powerlessness into your power space, take a moment to consider how power feels in your person. Think back to a time or instance when you felt powerful. Don't move forward until you have a moment coming to mind. The first thought popping into your mind might be your power moment.

SUMMARIZE YOUR POWERFUL FEELINGS. WHAT WORD OR WORDS CAPTURE IT?

Power feels different to different people. Power may not feel strong at all, or it might feel dominating. How do you know you feel powerful?

WHEN YOU IMAGINE YOURSELF IN THE POWER SPACE, WHAT IS HAPPENING? DRAW OR WRITE IT.

Feeling powerful may represent several characteristics and, when taken together, may form a larger vision or deeper connections evoking an image, object, smell, sound, or taste. Taking those sensations and discovering if there is a vision associated with your power can help distinguish power better.

WHAT COLOR IS YOUR POWER, IF ANY?

Your power may have a color associated with it. Power and powerlessness may be the same color. Power may have a different color or no color at all.

WHAT SHAPE DOES YOUR POWER POSSESS?

As you imagine your powerful self, a shape or feature may come to your mind.

HOW DO YOU KNOW YOUR POWERFUL SELF IS PRESENT?

This shape or feature may take on additional characteristics when you imagine your powerful self. A metaphor may come to your mind. Are you a powerful solid anchor? Do you envision a soft and light cloud? Does a rocking chair come to mind? What is distinctive and represents your powerful self?

DESCRIBE IN DETAIL ONE OR TWO OF THOSE WAYS TELLING YOU YOUR POWERFUL SELF IS PRESENT. DOES IT HAVE A MOTION? UP, DOWN, RIGHT, LEFT, AROUND, OR UNDER? IF IT'S STATIONARY, IS IT LIGHT, HEAVY, BIG, OR SMALL?

Certain features and characteristics manifest when your powerful self is present. Your shoulders may drop. You may be standing up. You might be running or breathing easily or heavily. In whatever way your powerful self shows up, consider how you recognize power is present.

PICK THE MOST VITAL SENSATION OF YOUR POWERFUL SELF. WHERE IS ITS SOURCE OF ORIGIN?

Your powerful self street address may be a location you have not considered. When you feel your powerful features, sensations, and feelings, they give rise to a place where these manifest for you. Where are these sensations the strongest for you? The location provides you with an indication of your power's origin.

SUMMARIZE WHAT YOUR POWERFUL SELF FEELS. PICTURE IT IN YOUR MIND, FEEL IT IN YOUR BODY, AND NOTICE IT IN YOUR SPIRIT.

From your cozy power home, consider all the features and characteristics of your powerful self. If you stray from your powerful self, review the prior questions and answers, allowing you to stay connected to your power biomarkers. Summarize all your power biomarkers to create your recipe.

IF YOU CAN SENSE POWER PRESENT AFTER EXPLORING THIS POWERFUL SPACE FOR YOURSELF, RECALL THE CHALLENGE YOU IDENTIFIED PREVIOUSLY. IF YOU DON'T FEEL YOUR POWER IS PRESENT, REVIEW YOUR POWER SUMMARY. WHAT INSIGHTS COME TO MIND FOR YOUR CHALLENGE?

You began considering a specific challenge where you felt your powerful self was lacking. In this powerful space you've created, insights may abound. Take this opportunity to reflect on your challenge and the wisdom arising for you when your powerful self is present. Go back to your power biomarkers while reflecting.

Your power biomarkers are the distinguishing features (shape, color, motion, smell, center, and sensations) you have discovered. When you rediscover your power, you may find new wisdom.

Remember Ashley, our marketing and media relations expert, dealing with the *jerk* from earlier?

For Ashley, a lack of power felt heavy, scattered, messy, and out of control. Ashley's powerless space looked similar to a canvas of splattered shards of multiple colors mashed up in a traffic accident. She felt organized, studied, crisp, and clean when we explored her power space. She even associated her power space with a linen smell. Her power space exuded calm and organization and was clean and welcoming.

ASHLEY'S POWER

Posture___*Sitting tall*___
Feels Like*Organized. Crisp. Clean*
Center____*Chest*_____
Motion*Small movements, welcoming*
Sensation*Smelled cleanliness*

Figure 1. Ashley's power recipe card.

In Ashley's power space, she found the unexpected. She discovered in this space a different perspective. Ashley recalled her executive, the jerk, asked her, "You have it ready, don't you?" In the past, this conjured up a frantic and out-of-control Ashley knowing for a fact she did not have *it* ready.

After her power assessment, she concluded, "What if the jerk *assumes I am* always prepared?"

Ashley realized *she* was the one with the power. Finding her power rocked her world. She began to see herself and others differently.

Ashley could envision the jerk being a scared little boy. She started seeing herself differently. She found the power to stand her ground against this little boy's expectations. She was able to take a few small steps toward reclaiming her power, her first step toward higher ground. Her next step was finding her voice and confidence in reclaiming her power.

POWER EXERCISE

You have several traits describing your power biomarkers. You can use these to create your power recipe card and note your power biomarkers.

POWER

Posture_____
Feels Like_____
Center_____
Motion_____
Sensation_____

Figure 2. Power recipe card. This is an empty power recipe card you can use to capture your power biomarkers, your posture, what power feels like, where power centers, any motion you notice, and any sensations you experience. Use this power recipe card for reference or practice later.

DISCOVERING YOUR POWER

What does power mean to you? Power is to possess or control authority or influence over people. Power is your source of energy, a wellspring of energy at your disposal to dispense.

Your power features and characteristics are unique. Your power looks and feels a certain way to you.

A power self-assessment can help you have a deeper understanding of how you communicate and exude power, and you'll begin to capture how your power manifests when you exude it. You can begin to practice making your power appear with your recipe card. The more you practice power, the better you will be at showing up with your authentic sense of power. Share your power with others.

A powerful recipe is one component of your power. The bedrock of your power lies in your ability to communicate with clarity, consistency, and confidence. How you communicate to others demonstrates your power, our next exploration.

CHAPTER FOUR

Powerful Communications

God speaks in the silence of the heart.

—MOTHER TERESA

If God is speaking, nobody's listening or, at best, distracted. Seventy-five percent of the time, we have distractions or pre-occupations, and we only remember about 20–25 percent of what we hear (Huseman 1991). However, nothing solidifies a powerful base better than powerful communication skills.

Conversations determine the health and productivity of the organization (Ramadhani 2020). Powerful communication determines the health and productivity of any institution, be it marriage, government, higher education systems, organizations, or society. When we communicate, we perceive we do it better than anyone else, as evidenced by an often-cited study, where nearly 100 percent of the participants said their communication skills were more effective than their colleagues

(Haney 1979). These statistics indicate that we are in 100 percent agreement. Our communication skills are poor at best.

Communication is more than stringing words together for a fluid, cohesive sentence. *Communicare* is the Latin origin for communicating, meaning to participate, impart or share, by implication to another, i.e., something or someone else (Durham Peters 2008). Listening is the bedrock of any powerful communicator. Don't believe me? Think of an instance when the most silent person in the room speaks up. It's been my experience that everyone turns to listen to the new tone vibrating in the room.

I think we tend to dismiss listening because many of us can hear. Perhaps we are being lulled into a false belief that hearing is listening. Maybe our deaf brothers and sisters have mastered listening because they tune into various sensations in their powerful communication toolkit to listen. Listening is the first language skill we acquire. However, we celebrate children's first words and not their first listening (Canpolat 2015).

Two weeks after a conversation, I struggled to recall what my client learned or took away from our last coaching conversation, regardless of how memorable the conversation was. Notes are invaluable at times. As someone trained in elite attention skills, I can attest that the better your attending skills are, the better a communicator you will be, regardless of how much you remember. We begin, therefore, with attending abilities.

ATTENDING

Communication occurs at different levels. Listening implies you are giving your attention to sound or action. *Attending* means being present or paying attention. You can attend with your nose, your eyes, your hands, your skin, your intuition, and let's not forget your ears. Have you ever tried attending to someone with your nose?

Neuroscientist John McGann reveals that the human sense of smell rivals or outperforms animals' sense of smell and may include the social spread of emotion through olfactory cues. If you thought the human sense of smell was poor, think again. Olfactory environments, McGann says, "can evoke strong emotional and behavioral reactions as well as prompt distinct memories" (McGann 2017). Something to ponder the next time you catch a whiff of dinner.

You can also attend with your eyes. When I travel to Scandinavia, I often listen or participate with my eyes because I don't speak the language. My Finnish hosts, Sanna and Karri, would welcome me into their home when I'd visit. They and the kids would converse. I would listen with my eyes. While one would address the other, a phrase similar to the following might be uttered:

"Oletkö menossa pyöräilemään vai patikoimaan huomenna."

I attended with my eyes and ears. By the tilt of the head and the change in tone, I understood it was a question awaiting a response. Through repetition and familiarity with certain words, I understood huomenna meant tomorrow. While I didn't understand the question, "Are you going biking or hiking tomorrow?" I learned a lot of Finnish by listening with my eyes and using my hearing differently. I learned to become less reliant on spoken words. When I did recognize words, it was after noticing visual cues. When I found words, it was similar to finding a gift or a surprise. My goal wasn't to find a word. My goal was to understand. Listening with your hands is similar.

When I walk Qui, our Mastweiler, around the neighborhood, his "vicious" growl can scare others. His "I'm scared" growl sounds different from his "back off" growl, and they both sound menacing. As we walked him one morning, the school crossing guard approached us holding the school crosswalk sign in front of his face. Qui growled, scaring the poor guard. The guard gave us a piece of his mind for owning such a vicious beast. I understood Qui's growl through the gentle reverberations of the leash in my hands. It was his "I'm scared" growl. To him, the crossing guard's head was floating in midair. When people scream and yell, we often don't question our other senses and miss cues from our hands, skin, or intuition.

According to Nobel Laureate Daniel Kahneman, "intuition is nothing more than recognition or gut instinct" (Kahneman 2011). Awareness of the body's inner state is interoception, using sensors within our bodies to send data to our brains (Paul 2021). Intuition, therefore, must rely on interoception as a communication vehicle. Becoming aware of interoception while doing anything else is near impossible and, if possible, takes practice.

Max, CEO of a growing company, talked nonstop for fifteen minutes after saying hello on our call. Max let me know he was having trouble with his board.

My first rule when working with any client is not to interrupt their initial dialogue. I always break it. Not interrupting is still my rule. My intuition and experience told me his topic might not involve the board. I stepped into my second rule, leading with silence before asking my simple question, "What's getting in your way here, Max?"

Max stopped and shared, "I'm a builder, and we've built. It's time for me to hand off the reigns to someone else, then I can build again. I'm fighting it."

When you allow for intuition, intuition will tell you what to say and when. However, you'll need to attend fully.

You can attend by listening for the words, the story, or the arc. Arc is a literary term for the path a story follows. Executive coaches and elite listening gurus are skilled in the listening arc. The listening arc is more than listening to the words. When listening to terms, the listener focuses on the words they are saying. When listening to the story, the listener intends to understand the story and the story's who, what, when, and why.

The listener isn't bound by the words alone when listening to the arc. Listening becomes a global observation of gestures, tone, silence, energy, terms, and emotions, and when it does is a special type of listening, arc listening. To arc listen, you are both near to the story and away from the story at the same time. Impossible, you say? Being near and far to the story takes practice and letting go of your wants, needs, interpretations, or even identifying similarities to your own life.

EDMUND

Edmund was frequently late to our calls and often interrupted by business needs. He seemed to have a habit of struggling to complete tasks. As CEO of a large company, he found it tough to hand off tasks to others because of his idiosyncrasies. Attending Edmund meant setting aside my struggles in handing off more functions to my assistants.

In conversing with Edmund, I shared a reframing tool I will share with you as well, "Edmund, when you are out doing the things anyone else can do, who is out doing what only you can do?"

Edmund stopped in his tracks. He had discovered his aha moment.

When you listen to the arc, you discover the person intimately. The arc tells about someone else's values, fears, wishes, wants, hopes, and dreams. When you listen to the arc, you can enter a conversation with a natural ease of knowing the person and connect with immediate authenticity. Arc listening requires you to set aside your needs, wants, and self. Edmund discovered he was hampering his progress. Finding that you are hindering your progress is easy. Doing the work of unhampering yourself is challenging.

Reflecting on my coaching later, I identified with Edmund's struggles. While I was further along in unhampering myself than Edmund, the conversation served as a reminder that I could strengthen my handing-off muscle by giving away more tasks and letting go of those tasks. The moment you judge the speaker, you are no longer arc listening or attending. To improve your attending skills, practice being able to notice your thoughts and set them aside. Meditation or prayer are both good practice moves for improving your attending skills.

ATTENDING TOOLS

Attending tools make your communication journey an adventure. The techniques below will make your listening journey a safari. Treat each approach similarly to different safari photos. Each is another animal or feature along the safari. Use them in conversations and explore how each one might sound when you add your personality. I've given a few examples of each technique.

SUMMARIZE

Summarizing is reflecting the essence of what you believe you heard.

"This all seems to point you in a new direction."
"You have a group you can influence. You aren't their leader and aren't responsible for them."

REFRAME

Reframing is reflecting and offering a different way of looking at something.

"Edmund, when you are out doing the things anyone else can do, who is doing what only you can do?"

"If you spoke to yourself as you do to your trainees, what would be different?"

"You seem to give everyone grace, acceptance, and understanding, except yourself."

PERSPECTIVE

Perspective sharing is sharing your viewpoint without attachment.

"You say you are looking forward to this. You don't look like it."

"You look uncomfortable."

"I've noticed we aren't on the same page anymore. What are your thoughts?"

"We seem to both be doing the same work. What might be a good way to split our efforts to accomplish more?"

INTUITION

Sharing intuition goes beyond what you hear and uses your senses.

"Something doesn't seem right."

"I feel as though we missed something."

"It's like something is different about our team now."

OBSERVATIONS

Share what you notice without attachment or judgment. Sharing observations allows you to connect with the speaker.

"It doesn't look like this is important for you right now."
"You love the mission of the organization."
"You're answering emails over the weekend, sending a message to the team that you expect them to work at all hours."
"You seem to interrupt others when you have something to say, and it's sending a message; only your message matters."

LANGUAGE PATTERNS

Adapt your language to the speaker's language and language patterns. This lets the speaker know you've been listening and allows them to hear themselves through your voice.

"I heard you're feeling overwhelmed. What can I take to relieve you?"
"What is different if your 'quirks' don't get in the way?

BODY LANGUAGE

Reflect on what nonverbal communication you see, helping the speaker see things they don't witness.

"What's the frown about?"
"You went all rigid when you mentioned Eric."

Notice that not all attending tools are questions. Repeated questioning leads to someone feeling interrogated. By using these different attending tools, you can create a rich conversation.

ATTENDING EXERCISES

Practice this exercise to strengthen your attending muscles.

1. Prepare yourself to attend to another human being. 'This human being with real wishes, fears, hopes, and anxieties is my focus.' Take a few deep breaths and set your needs aside to be present to someone else. Once you have taken a few deep breaths, celebrate with a smile or tell yourself, "I am great at attending to others." Repeat this often. You don't have to listen to someone as part of this exercise. This exercise prepares you to attend.

2. Write with pen and paper in your handwriting, "I listen for the arc." Typing fails to make the neural connections for cementing the memory needed for this exercise (Lotze 2014; Shah 2011; Umejima 2021). Write it out. Smile, raise your fist in celebration, or otherwise rejoice.

3. Practice attending with your ears to your spouse, children, grocery store worker, pharmacist, coworker, receptionist, or neighbor.

4. When you attend, before you respond, say something about what you heard using one of the attending tools presented. When finished, give yourself a wink for being a listening arc genius.

5. Explore one of the above tools when talking to someone on the phone. When you hang up, congratulate yourself. Being successful in attending is not a prerequisite. Over time, you'll succeed more. Continue rejoicing in the attempts.

COMMUNICATION

If you are like me, you might have a lot of inner dialogue. Often, I'm conversing with myself, processing the information I learned, similar to Ian Rutledge, Scotland Yard inspector, returning from the war with his dead officer, Hamish, as a voice in his head (Todd 2011). Having whispered conversations with myself, gesturing, pausing for silence, and waiting for a response makes me stand out. Often my husband will say, "How's Hamish doing?"

Whoops!

In these moments, I am figuring out how to share or impart knowledge to others. Before I share or impart knowledge to others, I must think about it with Hamish. My thinking can occur in muttered whispers with gestures. You don't need to carry on a conversation with Hamish to communicate effectively. Instead, you can use these four techniques to boost your communication skills: laser talk, metaphors, silence, and gestures, including a few exercises to develop your communication skills. Conversations and practicing with Hamish are optional.

LASER TALK

Direct communication is laser talk. Laser says it all. Laser is a metaphor saying direct communication. When you are in a safe space, saying what you mean with clarity is easy. In a political party, voicing your support for a candidate is easy because like-minded people surround you. In all other spaces, you might avoid expressing your beliefs to avoid standing out, starting a debate, or having your peers label you.

I find that my coaching clients don't struggle to say what they mean in a coaching conversation. I treasure what they say. They don't have to apologize for what they say or believe in a conversation with me. I treasure their words and do not judge them.

My clients often say, as Maureen, one of my clients, puzzled, "It's easy for me to speak here. How do I say it at work?"

Cultivate a zone of safety and comfort where people can speak the truth and words flow effortlessly. While laser talk requires confidence and power, we can explore several components of laser talk, revisiting after we explore your confidence in the presence chapter.

Maybe you think laser talk is impossible. Peter, one of my clients, is a storyteller. Anytime I ask Peter a question, his reply turns into a long yarn. I hear about his last place of employment, a past project, and the people working on the project. Some people are natural storytellers and think in terms of stories. Even Peter is capable of laser talk.

Think of a moment when you spoke with laser accuracy. For most people, at least one moment will come to mind. What enabled you to talk with laser precision?

The best way to develop your laser talk muscle is to use it in the easiest environments possible. However, some guidelines to know about laser talk can help you as you discover your unique laser talk flavor.

LASER BENEFITS

Laser talk can help keep meetings or a group on task. Introducing laser talk in a meeting lets us all keep declarations and points concise. Laser talk allows many voices to be part of the conversation. Keeping the conversation points concise will keep the energy and movement at a high pace. Meetings end on time when laser interactions are employed.

When I instigated laser talk as part of my meetings or as subsections of the meetings, everyone got to practice laser speaking. Laser moments contributed to higher pacing, reinvigorating the meetings. It also let people know we were attempting something new, meaning failure instead of perfection was okay. We rejoiced in the attempt, even the failures. We were trying to laser speak. Attempting laser communication served as a rejoicing moment with the team. Celebrating reinforces the concept that we are aiming for progress, not perfection.

LASER GUIDES

Not all conversations are appropriate for laser speaking. Use your wisdom in choosing your laser moment. Laser responses will offend someone sharing a deep, painful, or intimate experience. Employee development conversations are not times to work on your laser communication muscles. Some components of meetings are suitable spaces to explore laser communication. Laser talk for the entire discussion might be a bit aggressive. When you want a variety of input in a short amount of time, a laser section may be appropriate.

If you want to introduce laser communication to a group as part of a meeting, here is a brief guide to help you.

- Introduce the topic. "I've reserved ten minutes of our meeting today to listen to your topics for the next section call."
- Introduce the concept. "What I'd like for us to play with today is using laser speaking to make sure everyone has a chance to contribute."
- Introduce the boundaries. "Get your topic out with concise language and with the needed details, allowing us to understand your topic."
- Go, laser. "What's not clear?" or "Who is kicking us off?"
- Rejoice. Be grateful for the small wins and the attempt. People can get frightened of failure and hesitate to try new things. When you understand people change because they feel good about something, you realize rejoicing in the attempt is critical (Boyatzis 2019). You don't have to roll out a parade. You can say thanks and give appreciation to everyone trying this new skill (Fogg 2019).

METAPHORS

Metaphors have a way of holding the most truth in the least space.

—ORSON SCOTT CARD

Any communication toolkit would be incomplete without exploring metaphors. The previous section included a metaphor, laser talk. A laser is an amplified and concentrated beam of light, and when used to describe communication, laser represents the essence of what you are describing. Get to the point. One word, *laser,* communicates *get to the point.* Metaphors are a simple way to share clear and concise ideas and engage the senses and the imagination as a figure of speech applied to an object or action to which the word doesn't apply.

In fMRI experiments, neuroscientists have found expressions such as "grasp the idea" and "bend the rules" light up brain regions such as the somatosensory cortex involved with touch and feel. (Lai 2019) Using literal language does not. Participants have near-immediate activation of the sensory-motor region of the brain, suggesting that metaphors play a substantial role in comprehension and learning (Marangon 2016; Lai 2019).

METAPHOR BENEFITS

Metaphors also have a role to play in memory retention. Using metaphors is a proven aid for retention and recall. Engaging various parts of the brain also makes memories stickier by engaging different touch and sense areas of the body (Halonen 2021). You have a deep and rich experience with metaphors. Metaphors cement learning and make the memories stickier (Mills 2014).

METAPHOR GUIDES

I once confused salt with sugar when making lemonade. Salt is powerful. Being mindful of when you use it, how much to use, and questioning if what you are using is the right thing to use are practical considerations when working with ingredients. Salt in large quantities is not suitable for lemonade. Metaphors are the same. When overused, metaphors overwhelm your audience, and you risk losing them. Since metaphors are powerful, evoking several physical and emotional sensations, too many metaphors lead to sensory overload. Use metaphors when you want to

- Communicate a succinct point
- Relay an important point
- Ensure your audience recalls your point

My friend Jerry loves to speak in metaphors. He is a story-teller and loves to paint a vivid picture for himself and his audience. While preparing a high-level presentation for a potential collaborator, he spent hours crafting his presentation while working in isolation. After the presentation, when recapping, he demonstrated his slide, a photo of a three-pronged cactus in the desert. The arid three-armed cactus, he said, was "to show what working with me would be like." Proud of his three-pronged cactus showing the three different avenues of exploration the partners would navigate together, he missed the other thorn-ridden view, needling its way to at least my mind.

After he concluded, I inquired, "Jerry, which part of the cactus with all these needles in a desert represents your partnership?"

Silence. "I didn't look at the needles. I was looking at the cactus with three arms to show the three directions," he said.

"When I look at this, I see needles and a desert, not a hospitable place," I said.

"I didn't see this," he said.

When you use metaphors, consider the broader context or ramifications.

METAPHOR EXAMPLES

Often people struggle to think of metaphors. Chances are you have exercised metaphors in your day-to-day conversations and not noticed. We've used several in this section already. Using metaphors is a simple way to connect two, unlike things, making a connection or comparison between two things having no reason for being connected.

- "She has the heart of a lion." She can't possibly have the heart of a lion. Physiologically, we aren't compatible with lions. The metaphor captures that she is tenacious, brave, and will not give up easily.
- "He bent the rules." You can't bend the rules. Bending the rules means breaking them in an unimportant way.

- "What a soup sandwich!" A soup can't be a sandwich. A sandwich can't be soup. A soup sandwich paints a picture of something gone awry. It is all wrong.
- "My computer is a dinosaur." Dinosaurs once lived and are now extinct. Though less than fifty years old, your computer may seem outdated compared to this year's model.
- "I'm between a rock and a hard place." Unless you are rock climbing and find yourself wedged in a crevice, you are not between a rock and a hard place, although you may feel you are.

Play around and create metaphors. The world is your oyster when it comes to metaphors!

SILENCE

Nothing strengthens authority so much as silence.

—CHARLES DE GAULLE

In Finnish culture, silence is a cultural trait not of boredom instead of mutual respect and admiration. Silence is an integral part of the usual way of communicating in Finnish culture. Silence is the absence of words, the story between the spoken words.

When we fill the void between the spoken words, we lose the depth of the story. Often we fill the gap because we are uncomfortable. Silence can be discomforting until you take a step toward embracing silence and discover "the rest of the story," as Paul Harvey would say (Aurandt 1978).

SILENCE BENEFITS

At times silence is a relief not to have to fill the void with nonsensical words. If silence makes you anxious, the silence itself is not the culprit for what makes you cringe. The silence may remind you of a fear you carry of loneliness, being alone, the unknown, or something else associated with a void. Set your sights on embracing silent moments. It can be a moment.

- Take a walk in the woods and let the sounds of the unknown rise to meet you.
- Put down all your devices, take a deep breath and listen to your heartbeat.
- Silence will allow you to know yourself and love yourself better than any word could do for you.

A baby resting on someone's chest, with soft, quiet breathing, listening to the other's heartbeat, lulls the baby to sleep, and it's one huge unspoken love dialogue. Silence is powerful. Use it well.

SILENCE GUIDES

In the end, we will remember not the words of our enemies, but the silence of our friends.

—MARTIN LUTHER KING, JR.

Silence has a proper place and time. Righting an injustice or a wrong is the wrong place for silence. Your silence, in these instances, communicates volumes. Righting an injustice or a wrong requires heroic bravery. Silence on these occasions is cowardice.

When someone shares an intimate or emotional struggle, silence and inaction can be condemning.

"We got into an argument. She broke down crying, and I stood there. She ran out. It was awkward. What am I supposed to do?" Steve said. "I stood there unprepared for tears. I didn't say anything. I guess my face said it all because she ran out."

"When my friends cry, I sit down and invite them to sit and prepare myself to sit with them for a while, or I may hand them a tissue," I said.

"Oh," he said. "I didn't think it could be something easy."

A simple offering or gesture often makes a deep connection. Gestures can also make a deep connection between souls.

GESTURES

Gestures connect words with movement and add persuasive force to your communications to express an idea or meaning. Research shows gestures enhance memory, and gestures help us understand and express abstract ideas, be they spatial or relational (Paul 2021). Maybe moving your hands seems like random gesticulation. Moving your hands helps you and your audience think more intelligently. Gestures provide an alternate form of communication for you and your audience. Providing extra verbal meaning with gestures means gestures convey things we don't or can't say (Paul 2021).

Research shows that movement carries a sense of meaning. (Paul 2021). Meaning carries information critical to our thinking processes. Since memory for what you have heard is limiting, augmenting your memory by adding movement strengthens your memory and reinforces your audience's memory (Hostetter 2008). Similar to a metaphor, gestures tap into your prefrontal cortex and connect different somatosensory networks to create stronger hooks into your memory. Your memory and the memory of your audience augment (Özyürek 2014). Movement engages procedural memory. Declarative memory contains information (Paul 2021). Connecting movement with information activates both types of memory for yourself and your audience. Hence your recall is more accurate (Blake 2019).

When done with intention, connecting words to movement is another powerful tool for your communication arsenal. Slapping your hands around in an unmeasured manner is unhelpful. Therefore, train yourself, your speech, and your movements in coordinated unison. Otherwise, leave this tool outside of your communication arsenal. Gestures are too powerful a tool to wield haphazardly.

GESTICULATION EXERCISE

One way to practice gestures is to coordinate a single movement with a word or phrase. When you use the phrase or expression, trigger the action. For some people, this exercise will be easy. For others, the gesture exercise will be a struggle. If you struggle, consider the struggle a significant indicator not to exercise this tool without further assistance.

PERFECTION

Practice doesn't make perfect. As my good friend Tom says, "Practice makes permanent." The exercises and examples provided allow you to practice permanence, not perfection. Perfection is something we'll talk about next, along with common power pitfalls.

CHAPTER FIVE

Pitfalls and Perfect Power

We may succumb to powerlessness, helplessness, and victim-ization, but then we swing to the other extreme by aggressively wielding power over those around us.

—MELANIE BEATTIE

My dogs love to eat when we eat. When we sit at the dinner table without first putting his food bowl on the floor, Galen, the Irish Wolfhound, will whine in the middle of our meal. He's a social eater and wants the option to eat while we eat, even if he doesn't touch his food. We put his bowl on the floor before sitting down to eat because if we don't, we can't eat in peace, a pitfall. When you know what they are, you can avoid pitfalls. We will explore the most common power pitfalls. You can begin to recognize them and plan how you want to avoid your pitfalls.

CATS AND CARS

Maisy had a team to lead. She wasn't the official business leader. As the de facto leader for over a month, she told me, "I'm in a holding pattern until they name the leader. The work hasn't stopped. My hands feel tied because I can't ask people to deliver stuff for this project. I am not the lead!"

Waiting to act as the leader until she was named the leader left Maisy powerless, uncomfortable, and in doubt.

A new HR role seemed perfect for Ming. Ready to move into a VP position, she sought internal and external roles suitable for her. Another leader asked Ming, "Would you interview for our VP role? I'd love to have you on our team."

Ming applied and interviewed for the role. While awaiting the decision, she came to me for coaching and felt awful about her chances, abilities, and herself. Of her performance, Ming confided, "I outperform my peers, year after year. In my company, decision-makers passed me over for promotions. Promotions are hard to get. I'm frustrated and disappointed because I haven't achieved my promotion."

"What will your promotion tell you, Ming?" I wondered.

"My promotion will tell me I've accomplished my dream. It will also say I'm successful and can be proud."

Can you relate to either Ming or Maisy?

While studying for a master's degree in Physics, I learned of Schrödinger's cat. This famous and fictitious cat is part of a thought experiment to illustrate the paradox of quantum superposition. The paradox goes similar to this: a cat in a black box with a radioactive substance possibly triggers a poison from a Geiger counter. The cat is dead and alive until we know whether the Geiger counter releases the poison or doesn't release the poison (Schrödinger 1935). In both Ming and Maisy's cases, they didn't award a role. The reality they experienced resulted from believing they did not have the role, the dead cat. Both Ming and Maisy disregarded the cat might be alive.

If you suffer the same situation as Ming or Maisy, I'll point you to a nifty sales practice. Car dealers in certain regions allow buyers to drive home off the lot with an unpaid car. It's called 'spot delivery' because it helps ensure you, the new car owner, go away feeling you are a new car owner. As the owner, you no longer shop for other cars because you are the proud owner of a new vehicle. Wait! You haven't bought it yet. You, however, *feel* you are a new car owner. The dealer seals the deal with the paperwork signing set for a not-too-distant future date after you, as the *'owner,'* return to sign off on the sale.

DOUBT

Have you ever watched a dog try to make sense of something you said? Those ears go up, tilting their head in one direction and then the other. It's often because they feel confusion and perhaps are in doubt. Dogs aren't alone in second-guessing.

Our Mastweiler, Qui, is one of the most intelligent dogs we've ever owned. My son would swear under oath that Qui understands everything we say and believes the dog does graduate-level math in his head. When Qui hears "walk," "Chewy," or "nummies," he sits up straight and waits for his walk or his treats. When he hears words similar, he cocks his head to one side, then the other, not sure he heard "Chewy, chewy," the words causing him to salivate profusely. I said it. He's not quite sure. He waits to see if I'll repeat it.

We do the same thing. We wait to see if someone will support us or tell us we can do something we already know we can do. We wait for someone to say it to us.

In Maisy's case, I asked her, "When did you earn the title of a mother?"

"I don't know. I took it," she said. "I can take it."

With Ming stuck waiting to hear the outcome of her interviews, I asked, "Ming, what have you been telling yourself?"

She told me what she had told herself, "If I don't get the role, I will be disappointed in myself. It will mean I am a failure. I failed."

Her eyebrows shot up. "Ming, what did you realize?" I said.

Ming smiled. "I am not a failure. My company will have failed by not recognizing my talent and performance. I'm not the one who would have failed. They will be the failure. Thank you, Lizette!"

Ming feared she wouldn't get the role and found she had the job or didn't have the job. If she didn't have the job, she found she could be disappointed in herself or others. Being disappointed in herself didn't make sense, given the evidence. She and Maisy embraced their power in the unknown by making the unknown more known. Maisy and Ming were isolated and alone in their quandary, another potential pitfall. One Andrea faced.

ANDREA

Andrea, a high-performing physician, graduated early, began her residency, established her clinical practice, and made department head in record time. Her work ethic and keen mind are not uncommon in the medical profession, where physicians are exceptional. Physicians, in general, are the smartest in the class. Once you assemble them in a department, you have a high concentration of exceptional and talented individuals.

I had the pleasure of hearing Andrea at a medical panel of women physicians at a women's conference.

Andrea's joy wrapped itself in her practice and home life upon becoming a mother. She and her husband welcomed their son into their busy lives. However, Andrea's son suffered from a rare condition needing special medical attention outside Andrea's area of expertise.

"I kept my medical practice going. I kept doing my head-of-department activities and became my son's sole medical advocate. I didn't share any of this with my staff. I didn't let my husband help. Our marriage got close to falling apart. I could have let him help. It didn't matter what we had for lunch. Why did I have to take it all on myself?" Andrea said.

Andrea had gotten through life dependent on her exceptional individual performance. She treated her son's plight like any individual effort on a heroic scale.

"I became his sole advocate, provider, decider, and parent. I shut my husband out. I always relied on myself and wanted things done my way. Looking back, I should have gotten help. Years of medical training, studying, and a habit of independence lulled me into taking this on myself," Andrea said.

The dangerous minefield in any career is the *all-by-myself* minefield. People don't see the all-by-myself mentality as a minefield. All by myself can show up as a space of self-reliance, thinking, *I can do it myself,* or *Help is a weakness.* This mentality can result in burnout or near burnout, as it did for Andrea. Years later, she was still repairing the damage inflicted by shutting out help.

Research shows that on more than one occasion, team performance outpaces individual performers (Cummings 2014). While exceptional individual performers may come up with an excellent solution, they will lack in creativity what a team can produce, even amid stress (Shook 2019).

Stress amplifies you. Stress changes your physical and mental landscape through a whole host of neurochemical and biological effects, manifesting because of stress (Mayo Clinic Staff 2021). Stress amplifies how you respond in situations.

Emergency personnel undergo repeated training to respond to emergencies in predetermined ways. People in a team learn how to react as a team. When in an emergency, you want your responses to be measurable and automated and a team around you because a team is more potent than an individual.

Had Andrea nurtured a team or community to support her throughout her career, chances are she would have been able to have a network of supporters to assist her when she needed it most. Saying in hindsight, "I should have gotten help," when you hadn't built the habit of getting help is self-defeating. Andrea uncovered a process failure she dressed up and accepted as her failure. She hadn't made the behavior and habits to bring in a team. Saying, "Next time I'll get help," is empty if you don't practice the small steps toward changing how you respond when you need help the most. Asking, "who do I know I can ask to get help in place now," is empowering.

Avoid defeat. Embrace empowering.

IT TAKES A VILLAGE IDIOT

"This hot cocoa represents the end of our vacation money," said Shawn.

"How are we out of cash? We've only been here four hours?" inquired Gus.

"The American dollar was not as strong as I would have anticipated, Gus, which is why I had to put the whole thing on a credit card," explained Shawn.

"You don't have a credit card, Shawn!"

"I said *a* credit card, not my credit card. It's your card."
(Franks 2009, 00:01:58)

Shawn, the shrewd character on Psych, leveraged his wit to go on an expensive holiday, inviting his best friend to join him and using Gus's money to pay for the trip (Franks 2009, 00:01:58). Become shrewd and cunning as you embark on your career or rise in leadership. You don't need to dupe anyone. Use your wit to establish a habit of bringing others with you. You'll have more fun together with others. Your different approach to problems will be more creative than you could have ever imagined solo.

TOSHA

Getting help from others meant weakness to Tosha. Asking for help meant she would demonstrate to her boss that she didn't have what it took to solve the department's challenges. In one of our engagements, I helped Tosha find her approach in assisting one of her direct reports.

I asked Tosha, "Since you had to help someone from your team last time, what do you think of him and his performance?"

"Oh, good Lord. He's our best engineer. He had a challenging situation where two people were better than one. I enjoyed working with him," reflected Tosha. "Hmmm. I guess my boss sees me the same way. I'll see him when we're done," she said.

THE CIRCLE OF LIFE

In this game of life, no one should walk it alone. In your career, you will need help, you will be someone else's help, and occasionally, you will be the cause of someone needing help. When navigating your career, you may want to seek peer support, a sponsor or advocate to help lift you, be a protégé to someone or be part of a supportive community.

When I work with my clients to identify a sponsor or advocate for them, we tend to touch on what good sponsor or advocate attributes are. If you want to know what a good sponsor or advocate is, be one for someone else.

PERFECT POWER

It is good to have an end to journey toward; but it is the journey that matters in the end.

—URSULA K. LE GUIN

When I was learning how to close a suture, I wanted to ensure I got it perfect. I wanted to ensure my entry, angle, and looping were perfect, as shown in the textbook. Closing the suture too tight meant I had to repeat my sutures. The enemy of good isn't bad; it's better. Good may be what the need is.

SCHOOLWORK AND WORKPLACE WORK

In school, we aim for perfection and teachers reward us for it. Score perfect on exams and scholarships open for you. If you do well, you are honored and admired on the honor roll, honor society, dean's list, valedictorian, and on. Perhaps someone calls on you to highlight your excellent work, and you walk away, pleased you are doing the things you should be doing for success.

Schoolwork is crucial for helping us learn. Scoring the highest marks can turn into an end in itself. When and if we focus on the grades, we miss the point of learning. We praise the scores and the grades when we should honor the learning. You might need a fair to a good understanding of the material to put the knowledge into practice. Education isn't bad. I have a PhD and fond respect for academic pursuits. When prizes in learning become the coveted item, I have missed the point of the learning quest.

In graduate school training, failure is part of learning. Students learn to experiment, test, and form a hypothesis, among other things. The purpose of the experiment isn't success. The purpose is knowledge. Learning is what happens in failure, a painful and necessary step.

HERMIONE

Meet Hermione, who is working for a large organization. She had worked there for over fifteen years. Hermione's outstanding contributions at work advanced her into a leadership development program. She lacked her desired promotion.

In parallel to her career, Hermione applied to an Ivy League school leadership development program with the approval of her organization. They admitted her.

Hermione told me, "I was interested in the training because I've been in my division for years and wanted to move up. Promotions are rare in my organization. I'm the only Black woman in our entire division. Women are rare in my field. We had a position for a director, and my boss sourced a candidate from outside the organization. The candidate had less experience and knowledge of our field than I had."

When Hermione and I met for coaching, the outside candidate had already entered her workplace as a colleague. He was in the director role Hermione had hoped to have.

"I completed the Ivy League training, scored high in all the coursework, and I don't understand why I can't make the leadership development training work for me. I am the only provider for my family, and I don't want to rock the boat and risk losing my job," Hermione said.

She had the knowledge, experience, and training to succeed. Her tone spoke her frustration. She learned a powerful lesson about the differences between the classroom and real life. What Hermione was searching for from our coaching were poise tools. We'll address poise tools in the following few chapters.

Doing homework and schoolwork well doesn't mean you are prepared to actualize and live out the learning. Indeed, the lesson and the schoolwork are one component of the learning journey. People may excel at the initial learning journey and disregard the middle and ending bits. Putting into practice mistakes, failures, course corrections, feedback loops, building habits, and mastery are the next steps in sealing your career advancement potential with or without schoolwork.

ADVOCATING FOR YOURSELF

Hermione expected rewards for her excellent work as she received recognition in school. The workplace is not the schoolyard. When her workplace efforts failed to convert into promotions in the workplace, she resented her employer and her boss and felt overlooked. However, she didn't discuss her aspirations with her leader. She didn't know how to have the conversation. She didn't have the conversation. She felt her accomplishments spoke for themselves and didn't talk about them or her aspirations with her leaders.

Leaving her employer didn't feel comfortable for her. Braving the great unknown filled her with trepidation and felt too risky, given she was the primary earner. Entertaining a conversation with her boss felt uncomfortable and scary, making her feel stuck between a rock and a hard place, unable to move, advance, or feel appreciated where she was. If conversations similar to this perplex you, here is a simple model I've modified from coaching various groups. You can use this framework to have a feedback conversation with your leader. It may work for you as it did for Hermione:

- "Here are what I believe are my accomplishments." List them out. "Did I miss anything?"
- "This is what I believe I should develop or focus on for my next step toward my goal(s) of _____." List them out. "What have I missed? "

- "I am aiming for my next role of _____.
  What haven't I considered?"
- "Here is what I believe I need from you to get there." Be
  specific about your needs. "How can you support me?"

Leaders are navigating their careers with their leaders not
taking time to discuss their careers. Your leaders may be
jumping over their hurdles. They may want to help you. Your
leader may not know how. Not everyone aspires to leadership.
When you are clear about your needs, desires, and wants,
you guide your leaders to support you. Clear is kind (Brown
2018). If your leaders are not helping you after requesting
their assistance, you need to have a different conversation
and route. You won't know until you ask first.

POWERFUL VISION

Difficulties in advocating for yourself may trace back to one
reason. Meet Anna, a female leader seeking coaching because
she doesn't "have the confidence to find the words to talk to
her boss about her career development."

I asked Anna, "What would you do if you saw a child in front
of you run into a busy intersection?"

She said, "I run after the tyke in a heartbeat."

"What if your colleague struggled with their development
discussion with their boss? What would you do then?" I said.

"I'd hop in to have the discussion for them or join them to
meet with their boss," she said.

"You're struggling to have the conversation for yourself. What's different?"

If Anna could discard herself to save a child and put her discomfort aside to negotiate with someone's boss, she didn't suffer a lack of confidence. She had too narrow a focus. What Anna thought was a confidence problem was a vision problem. I struggle with myopic vision too. Advocating for myself is not natural.

When I prepared for my first power, poise, and presence group workshop, I had an appealing description of the program. The program flier lacked one major component, the director. The instructor is an essential component of any training program. The informational sheet didn't list her qualifications, credentials, or name. What gave the person the authority to conduct such a course? When people want to know you, it's not bragging to tell them who you are.

It's not showing off to tell people about yourself.

I have PhD training from the Mayo Clinic. I have executive coach credentialing through the International Coaching Federation. If showing your credentials is showing off in someone's view, they have a problem, not me. When I struggle to tell someone about myself, it's not a confidence problem. I hold too narrow a vision when I won't talk about myself. I need to see what others need to know about me and then share it as I would with a friend.

Showing off is saying, "I have a PhD, and you don't" or "What do you know? You don't have a coaching credential?" Both are judgment statements. Those statements treat people like things. We should use things and show people love.

In the example of Anna running into traffic, when she's running into traffic headlong or helping a colleague, her vision is on the person or the challenge the person is facing and how she can help. When she's afraid to talk to her boss or others about her career, her vision is a narrow focus on her discomfort. Running screaming into traffic to save another is uncomfortable and dangerous, and she saw beyond discomfort and danger to imagine doing what needed doing. What would change for you if you saw beyond your discomfort?

When you see beyond your discomfort, you have power vision. When your eyesight is myopic, you get glasses to help you see clearly. A coach or a thought partner might be an excellent set of spectacles for you.

Aim for power vision instead of tunnel vision.

POWER TOUCH
In one of my graduate training courses, the material challenged me to grow and learn. I struggled to grasp all the concepts. A few times a month, a group of students would meet for a study session.

Several of us struggled to understand the lectures. This specific course and content weren't crucial for overall success.

"Did anyone understand what he meant by the turbulence modeling part of the lecture?" I said.

Joe recounted in a relaxed fashion, "I don't know. I think I fell asleep."

After waking up and going through my morning routine, my sleepy haze disappears, revealing the majestic clarity of my overnight epiphanies. Joe's sleepy admission was the clarity I needed for change. I saw a whole new world where I could sit back and relax during lectures.

I have since learned to sit back and relax all the time, in lectures, in the board room, and in coaching calls. I find I'm far better prepared, approachable, and less demanding of myself when I do so. When I relax, I find I give the amount of powerful presence needed, and I'm far more confident in my conversations. Who doesn't enjoy approaching someone relaxed?

What I discovered when I lightened up changed my outlook on all my conversations and actions. My goal became determining the level of effort I should be giving. I had gotten complacent and treated all moments the same. Being intentional about what level of effort I need to put forth makes a massive difference in my success and productivity. I'm not saying you need to sleep in your meetings, board calls, or leadership team meetings. However, if you've tried everything else, why not give relaxing into it a try?

POWERFUL CLARITY
Joe's sleeping taught me a vital lesson. Knowing that not all things are equal gives you powerful clarity. An influential

leader doesn't treat everything with equality, not meriting equality. People are not things (Heuss 1955).

Powerful clarity is recognizing that not all things or activities are equal.

Treat things with inequality as merited. Treat all people with love.

A TIGHT GRIP

Our first Irish Wolfhound, a rescue dog we picked up when he was six, was a senior. Wolfhounds have a life expectancy of eight years old. He was lonely. A young couple, both physicians, returned a pup to the breeder when they couldn't give him any attention after starting a family. MacGregor needed a new home. Aside from wolfhounds being a giant breed of dog, they imprint on their human, forming a solid bond with their owner, similar to a two-year-old refusing to leave their mother's side. When we rescued Mackie, he weighed 120 pounds, a good sign of average weight. We didn't know much about his past when we rescued him. We learned it the hard way.

Within a week after we rescued Mackie, we took both of our dogs for a walk. Qui, the Mastweiler, has training as a puppy to walk at our right side next to his handler's hip pocket. We enjoyed our walks as a time to ponder, relax and consider or plan our days.

Excited and panting, both dogs were eager for us to leash them, and we walked out the door with my husband taking

Qui. Mackie was nothing less than a complete disaster as soon as we walked out the door. At 120 pounds, he dragged and yanked me down the street. Qui looked at this fool of a dog we had brought home with an expression I can only describe as "what are you doing?"

Mackie and I were a tangle of the leash, dog, and human, doing a dragging dance. I was pulling. He dragged me, and I tripped with jerking, walking, and running motions. It was a ridiculous dance.

All four of Mackie's paws were working overtime and trotting like I had four legs. For his part, I can imagine he wondered why on earth I was holding him back. We got to the end of the block, and for whatever reason, I thought I would get him under control. I turned the next corner with a tight grip on his leash, pulling and being pulled.

Halfway dancing down the next street, exhausted and worn out, I had to return home. When we got home, I needed a rest. I'm out of practice as a dog dancer. We had gone a total of fewer than three blocks, and my tight grip and the constant tug of war exhausted me.

My expectation of Mackie being a great walker, similar to Qui, ended up being a fantasy. I didn't stop to consider that he had no idea how to walk with people or the possibility that he had not been on regular walks. With too tight a grip, my hands, arms, and expectations felt exhausted in no time.

A WEAK GRIP

The next day with lowered expectations, we again set out the door. During this second venture out the door, I emerged with different expectations. We weren't planning to go any further than our street. I loosened my grip, and we walked at a trudging and slow pace. Anytime Mackie got ahead of me, I stopped.

He looked at me, somewhat puzzled. When he settled down, we were moving again or picking up the pace. As soon as he launched ahead of me, we stopped. He paused, gazing back at me, learning. When he slowed to my pace, I'd pick up the pace or vary our rate. Staying closer to my pace and watching me, we walked a healthy circuit.

Besides being a giant dog breed, wolfhounds are fast learners and seem to connect the dots behind whatever it is you try to teach them. Anything I taught him, he learned fast, faster than any other dog we'd ever owned. Whether he wanted to do what he learned is a different story.

We soon learned how to walk together, and he became an easy walking buddy. We soon traveled and hiked together, the best of companions, side by side, and we made it much further than three blocks.

It's okay to loosen your grip and soften your expectations if it makes your journey easier.

POWERFUL POISE

My death grip on the leash made my initial dog walking experience with Mackie rough on him and me. When I relaxed and tuned into Mackie, I could sense his carefree freedom, a new experience for him to have a partner and someone wanting to connect with him. He developed a deep love for me and our walks.

When you can balance your wants, wishes, and desires and join the conversation with the right expectations or with a loose grip, you lead in a productive way, energizing and refreshing you and those you lead, regardless of the difficulties or obstacles involved.

When you find your mix of power, whether in a group or a meeting, you can relax, be a part of the conversation and not be a part of the conversation. Powerful poise delivers the needed amount of effort when required and not a drop more. Poise embraces both effort and ease, something we'll discuss next.

POISE

CHAPTER SIX

Poise

———

Refusing to ask for help when you need it is refusing someone the chance to be helpful.

—RIC OCASEK

If you've ever watched a gymnast on the balance beam, jumping and twirling while maintaining their composure, you've seen poise. In your journey through life, you have a high probability of witnessing its opposite when gymnasts have fallen off, split the beam, or worse. I find the pommel horse for men and the balance beam for ladies the most nerve-racking gymnastic events because those are the events where even small mistakes become prominent and painful to watch. Poise is your ability to remain calm and composed regardless of the situation. When you have poise, your state of being, not necessarily your body, holds and exudes balance and equilibrium.

Having poise is the ability to fall flat on your butt and get back up, a smile on your face to continue without skipping a beat. For my client Sam, poise didn't look at all according to her imagination.

A HOUSE ON FIRE

"A bit of a house on fire," giggled Sam, my Australian client, when I asked how she was coming into our call.

Sam, a high-energy, forward-thinking leader, served as the project manager for a small nonprofit organization. Her nervous giggle spoke her first biomarker.

"Lizette, my board runs the organization the same way as if the pandemic didn't happen. Our major donor event is two weeks away, and I am getting pushback for why we aren't near our campaign goal. Why haven't the prospective donors I've courted not donated? It takes time to build these relationships. Anytime I try something new and innovative, the board gets grumpy," she said.

"Raise money for the hospital." She air quoted.

"I have been working to shift us into new and exciting areas. No one wants to hear what I have to say. Other nonprofits similar to us didn't make it through the pandemic. When I propose something new, the stodgy old board pushes back. I have a few backing me. I've also got a grumpy board member threatening not to donate if I keep up the new direction," she said.

Grumpy and Stodgy are getting in her way, I thought. I also picked up on her shallow breathing, tightening shoulders, and shrinking composure.

"If I don't help the organization shift, they are dead. If I help them shift, I've got members threatening to kill it. I've got this big donation event in a few weeks, and I am panicking," she coughed.

Another possible biomarker, I thought.

"I have a lot to do. I have Grumpy and Stodgy backing me into a corner. I want to go and hide. This donation event is going to be a disaster. I don't know what to do. I need you to help me calm the farm," she said while hacking and coughing.

Sam's organization didn't have a CEO. The established board ran the organization the same way for years, with the potential of not surviving the pandemic. Sam was panicking and knew she needed to "calm the farm," Australian slang for calm down. This is what Sam brought to coaching. What we discovered together was Sam's poise.

Sam's Biomarkers

Figure 1. Sam's biomarkers. In my conversation with Sam, these were the biomarkers I noticed during our conversation as she explained her dilemma.

We'll start in your space of needing to "calm the farm" when you aren't calm, allowing us to explore better the area where you feel relaxed and composed. We'll revisit what Sam found along the way.

POISE ASSESSMENT

Find a quiet space to ponder your assessment. Please turn off distractions, take a deep breath and get ready to explore poise and its opposite. Take your time in completing this entire section.

LACK OF POISE

WHAT IS A CHALLENGE YOU ARE FACING NOW WHERE YOU ARE MISSING POISE?

Challenges can feel defeating and leave us feeling off-balance, in a tizzy, or questioning ourselves. We get stuck being off-balance, perhaps during a challenging opportunity. What is your biggest poise challenge?

WHAT DOES A LACK OF POISE LEAVE YOU FEELING?

Various sensations can signal your poise vanishes. Curiously, a few sensations may signal the moment before your calm and balanced demeanor disappears. Different bodily sensations, emotions, memories, or fears can emerge. What happens to you?

WHEN YOU IMAGINE YOURSELF IN A SPACE WITHOUT POISE, WHAT DO YOU EXPERIENCE?

Specific activities may become impossible, or you may be rooted. You may feel light, off balanced, confused, or lost.

DOES IT HAVE A COLOR? A SMELL? A SHAPE? A TEXTURE? A NAME?

Think about what color, smell, shape, or size your lack of poise possesses.

WHAT SENSATIONS DO THE OPPOSITE OF POISE PROVOKE?

Staying with the sensations when you lack poise may seem difficult. There is richness in exploring this space from a non-judgmental point of view. Without judgment or attachment, notice what feelings link this space for you.

DESCRIBE ONE OR TWO OF THOSE SENSATIONS MORE.

Try to dig deeper into the strongest of those sensations. What does this sensation remind you of most? It could be that there is a memory attached to the sensation. Notice and describe it.

PICK THE MOST VITAL SENSATION. WHERE IS ITS SOURCE OF ORIGIN OR CENTER?

Try to dig with the curiosity of an archaeologist, gently probing and excavating this sensation to find its center.

SUMMARIZE WHAT THE OPPOSITE OF POISE CAUSES YOU TO EXPERIENCE.

Summaries are good for capturing all your explorations into a brief statement. While you are summarizing, something new may emerge. Jot it down.

FROM THIS SPACE LACKING POISE, WHAT MANNERISMS AND BEHAVIORS DO YOU SEE?

Exploring this space, you might see new observations. Note them without judgment or attachment, how a scientist would take note while peering into Petri dishes.

POISE

Switching into your space of poise, take a moment to consider how poise feels in your person. If you struggle, find an event or experience where you showed up with poise. Your experience doesn't have to be perfect or positive.

SUMMARIZE WHAT POISE CAUSES YOU TO FEEL.

When you envision yourself filled with poise, take a moment to consider what sensations are present.

WHEN YOU CONSIDER YOURSELF IN THE SPACE OF POISE, WHAT HAPPENS?

Sensations can be felt, experienced, or imagined and are a source of important information. This information may be a word, picture, or idea. Use your creativity to capture it.

WHAT IS YOUR POSTURE WHEN YOU ARE IN THE SPACE OF POISE?

Posture may seem unimportant to you. The shape your body makes may provide you with essential information to unlock hidden aspects of your poise.

WHAT EMOTIONS ARE PRESENT?

Take one or two of those emotions and describe them in detail.

TAKING THE STRONGEST SENSATIONS OF YOUR POISED SELF, WHAT EMERGES FOR YOU WHEN YOU CONSIDER ITS SOURCE OF ORIGIN?

Your poise home can be in multiple locations, mobile or stationary. Where is it for you?

WHAT DOES POISE CAUSE YOU TO EXPERIENCE?

Summarize your poise biomarkers. If you are in a space with poise, consider your challenging situation again and ponder what options arise for you in this newfound poise space. New ideas or avenues may have opened where before there were none. Please take note of them and jot down a few of them. Reflect on your poise biomarkers if you are not in your poise space.

What insights do you have about your poise challenge?

SAM'S JOURNEY

You may recall that Sam wanted to calm the farm. Sam loved her nonprofit organization. She loved the mission and vision she helped craft. As we uncovered Sam's topic, what stood out was that Sam was not comfortable in the space of not knowing, not knowing if the donors would bolt, not knowing if the board was fully supporting her, and not knowing if the major donation event of the year, she was organizing would be successful.

"Sam, with all you have going on, it seems grumpy is going to be grumpy," I said.

Sam got this far-away look and sat back.

"What's happening, Sam?" I said.

"Grumpy is going to be grumpy. It doesn't matter what I do. Grumpy is going to be grumpy! I know exactly what to do," she said.

"I know how to run a campaign. I have a few things hanging over me I need to tie off. I have to say no. I have other obstacles getting in my way. I feel the weight of the campaign and the whole organization before me. I must look at my work as if it's external and be dispassionate about it," she said.

"I need to release my grip, the whole thing, release my grip on the whole thing. This would help me in all aspects because then I can look at the whole thing and say, okay, is this worth it? Does this work for me? Does it not? That's interesting," she said.

"What changed here for you?" I wondered.

Sam shared, "I felt a sense of relief. I don't have to worry about it all the time. I can treat it with the mentality of doing a job. I'm letting go of the emotional entanglement. This campaign may or may not work. This role may or may not work. I'm getting more options—a bit more freedom. I've found a loose grip and more space to do the needed stuff. An ability to breathe a little more of completing the campaign and reevaluating my options on the other end for a new or different role outside of the organization."

Sam found her calm, poised, and balanced self where she didn't know the event's outcome and wouldn't know the outcome until afterward. She found a way to stay present with her discomfort, focus on the tasks she needed to complete, and release the result of the annual event from her worries as if the outcome didn't matter. She discovered she had options outside of the organization, and she could explore those options *after* the campaign. Whether she ultimately decided to stay or go, she found her options.

Sam's poise assessment revealed easy breathing, standing tall, holding on loosely to her ideas, comfort with risk, laughter, a larger vision she couldn't even grasp completely, and knowing her role in the vision, even with lacking clarity around her role. She also discovered she didn't need to see the outcome to know her options.

You can use an empty recipe card to capture your poise biomarkers.

SAM'S POISE

Posture Standing Tall
Feels Like Larger Vision
Center Easy Breathing chest
Motion Comfort with Risk Loose grip
Sensation Laughter

Figure 2. Sam's Poise Recipe Card. Sam's poise biomarkers were standing tall, having a larger vision, easy breathing centered at her chest, comfort with risk, a loose grip, and laughter.

"Lizette, I really leaned into the whole biomarker concept and was unflappable. I enjoyed it. We smashed it. The campaign was a huge success. Thank you." Sam beamed on our next call.

Sam found her inner calm and poise. Sam's poise biomarkers weren't the only tools she wielded that day.

POISE

Posture_____

Feels Like_____

Center_____

Motion_____

Sensation_____

Figure 3. A Poise recipe card. Use the recipe card to list your poise biomarkers. Refer to your biomarker recipe card to practice making your poise appear by experiencing your biomarkers.

CHAPTER SEVEN

Poise Tools

All our dreams can come true if we dare to pursue them.

—WALT DISNEY

When gymnasts first learn the balance beam, they practice on the floor with a floor tracing of a balance beam. They mature to a balance beam placed on the floor, then to a beam suspended above the floor to varying heights until they can compete on a balance beam at competition height. Only with advanced practice do they graduate to higher levels of beam work and always with mats and supervision.

We often want to go straight to beam work without the necessary skill built on the floor. When we cannot do an elevated level of mastery, a certain skill or task, we tell ourselves awful stories. The worst part is that we believe those horrible stories. In gymnastics, they practice challenging skills on the equipment with soft mats dulling the impact of falls. Falls are the expectation. Poise becomes better during times of adversity. You can use cushions to soften your fall. Start with small challenges to build the muscles needed to overcome the more significant challenges. To do this, we'll start with small tools for your poise toolbox before taking to the beam work with soft mats.

We start our tour of tools by first exploring the concept of resiliency, your cushions. Resiliency is bouncing back after a difficulty or a setback. It's the skill we all need and the one you'll need the most whether you rise into leadership roles or not.

RESILIENCY BENEFITS

Resiliency benefits you and others through better mental health, immunity, and lower blood pressure. Resiliency is a renewal process modulating the parasympathetic nervous system. Resiliency activities stimulate the vagus nerve, releasing oxytocin in females and vasopressin in males, helping your blood pressure to drop, helping your breathing to slow down, and your heart rate to slow (Boyatzis 2019). Various renewal activities can slow your breathing, lower your blood pressure, and heart rate, and bring multiple benefits to your stress-handling abilities.

RESILIENCY ACTIVITIES

Triggering resiliency can be done in various ways. A few essential techniques you might try are:

1. Dreams and visions: Spend time thinking or planning your future.
2. Walking in nature: Nature connects you to a larger vision of the world and can trigger your parasympathetic nervous system into action.

3. Mindfulness or praying to a loving God: Be aware of yourself and others. Pray or meditate. These activities can help build your resiliency.
4. Listening to orchestra music.
5. Helping conversations or coaching relationships.
6. Exercise
7. Yoga
8. Artwork and doodling
9. Daydreaming
10. Gardening

This list is by no means exhaustive. You can engage in several activities to trigger your renewal network. The key to renewing yourself and having resiliency is spreading it out. During sleep, your body has a sleep cycle, including periods of wakefulness, light sleep, deep sleep, and REM sleep. Even in sleep, we have variable activities. If you plot your sleep cycle out, the cycle resembles a waveform cresting, falling, and rising again. Our night cycle is no different from our day cycle (Walker 2017).

The design of our brains will cycle from higher activities to lower restful periods of activities, even during the day. This is the way we progress to optimal performance. Similar to a sleep cycle, building in periods of rest and renewal throughout the day is the best way to ensure you operate at peak performance.

Weave in renewal breaks in your day of heavy meetings, deep thinking, decision-making, and planning. I recommend that my clients take a twenty-minute break for ninety minutes of serious thinking, decision-making, meetings, or work.

Anything less, and you start burning more fuel for less mileage. With renewal breaks spread throughout your day, you can recharge and even push your efficiency higher than if you push through with sheer willpower.

ELITE RESILIENCY

Athletes and Elite athletes call it rest and recovery. During this rest and recovery period, essential work is happening. For athletes, toxins, cellular waste, and debris clear out, and muscles build and strengthen (Sprundel 2021). A similar phenomenon happens for the rest of us: mental clutter clears out, new ideas take shape, dots start to connect, easier paths emerge, and mental clarity improves.

When we forbid renewal from occurring, burnout happens. When people work their brains into thinking all day, deciding, planning, meeting, and executing, the brain doesn't get an opportunity to rest. While your brain is a computational entity, it is not a machine capable of switching off. Your brain cycles from higher energy activities to lower energy activities (Walker 2017). When you don't let cycling happen, things go haywire. You can find yourself in bed, unable to sleep, spinning, or on vacation, unable to disconnect from work.

Mental breaks are good mental fitness practices for your brain. This renewal gives you more creativity and awareness. The renewal allows endurance athletes to outperform their competition. Exercise performance scientists studied the effect of mental fatigue on endurance athletes and discovered that mental fatigue alone affected elite athletes' motivation and perception of effort.

The mentally fatigued elite athletes gave up earlier on endurance activities and had higher effort level perceptions than their peers (Meijin 2019). Being mentally exhausted made the athletes think the exercise was strenuous, and they quit earlier than their mentally fresh peers. Making a habit of taking breaks will improve your efficiency and mental balance and might leave you feeling your workday was pretty light.

Renewal breaks are one method to build your resiliency. There are other tools.

SELF-CARE MAMA BEAR

"Sorry, I'm a few minutes late. I'm exhausted," said Wendy as she dialed into our call.

In an earlier conversation, Wendy told me she was a recovering people pleaser.

"I've been trying to do better for my self-care. This well-developed, external mama bear tries to protect everyone important to me. The mama bear says, 'Oh, I get to come out of my cave now? I've been hibernating because she doesn't use me. I get to eat salmon and get fat now?' She's a little puny. I think she's showing up a little bit more, and, honestly, she's the one saying, 'Don't even engage with these guys. Don't. Don't even start with them because they're draining. They're exhausting. They don't do the right thing.'" Wendy said.

"Self-care mama bear is that great Aunt I didn't have who says, 'F*** if I care. I didn't want you bothering me with your silly little problems and bickering, but here's a cookie. I'm making amazing Osso Bucco later, and we can have tea and play cards.' You know, caring and engaged but not putting up with nonsense. 'Why are you making time for this nonsense, girlfriend?' She's a super warm and bigger lady who's pestered. 'You don't know my life and what I've been through, which is why I have no time for your nonsense!' No time for the nonsense!" Wendy said.

"And I wonder if there are other aspects of unraveling this fear. I'm not allowed to do what's best for me without weighing what's best for everyone else first, the people-pleasing. It's also 'I told you to do a thing. You better be compliant.' I don't know if I make sense, but it feels like there are those two aspects of authority figures. I am fighting the concept that we are to obey our elders." Wendy said.

"And self-care mama bear says?" I said.

"What, what elders? You're the elder now," Wendy realized mama bear was telling her.

Mama bear was a bigger-than-life character. She had a strong voice, a personality you don't want to mess with on a good or a bad day. Mama bear didn't give a thought, care, concern, or worry about what anyone thought. Mama bear had confidence in herself and could be strong and even bold, and she would also fix you a plate of cookies and have tea with you. Mama bear held boundaries firm and intact. When mama bear tried to come out to protect people-pleasing Wendy, mama bear found herself in a corner and told to take a nap. Mama bear wanted to come out. Wendy realized she wasn't letting her.

As soon as we identified mama bear, she entered our coaching space as a third party and became Wendy's trusted advocate.

In later coaching sessions, Wendy would smile at me, saying, "Mama bear came out to protect my time."

Mama bear is an excellent example of Wendy's resiliency. You have internal resiliency resources. Your internal resources may generate something in a different direction from Wendy's. I've found that each person has wisdom and experience, and when explored with a coach, they can manifest into a unique resiliency partner lasting a lifetime.

It's my honor to help others discover their lifelong resiliency buddy.

FREEDOM TO

When my seven-year-old son lugged grocery bags from the car to our house, his droopy shoulders signaled his heavy burden. As dad passed him walking back to the car, our son quipped, "Help me!"

His Papa responded, "Grow stronger."

In my son's cry for help, he had gotten help, not how he expected. He had a choice. He was free to drop the bags and take them one at a time. He could drop the bags and walk away. He could take the advice, lean into and on himself and continue to deliver the bags the best he could, growing stronger in the process. This is an example of *freedom to* or what others call *agency*. Agency means you have the capacity and the freedom to decide for yourself and your future (Frie 2008). With total freedom, he chose to heave the bags over his shoulder, straighten up, and finish his grocery delivery journey.

Fast forward a few weeks later when a similar grocery hauling event occurred: This time, his five-year-old sister struggled to haul a bag of groceries from the store to the car. She cried to her older brother for help. He looked straight at her and repeated the advice given to him, "Grow stronger." Incredulous, she glared back and made her decision with complete freedom. She heaved the bag on her back and finished her grocery delivery route. The seven-year-old had learned agency and had provided it to his sister.

Years later, I'm happy little gets in her way. She tackles most anything because she thinks she can. We nurtured her belief in herself to affect change and have the *freedom to* decide independently. She has indeed grown stronger.

Resiliency and agency overlap, build, and cultivate each other. In good times you can develop agency before resiliency. In tough times, it's difficult to experience defeat and believe you have the *freedom to* choose. This, however, is what Victor Frankl observed and documented during his imprisonment.

FREEDOM TO CHOOSE

Victor Frankl wrote about his Nazi concentration camp experience in *Man's Search for Meaning.*

As a prisoner and trained psychotherapist in a Nazi concentration camp, Dr. Frankl used his psychotherapy training to work with prisoners to identify a purpose in life they could feel optimistic about. He immersed them in imagination to a purposeful outcome, despite the bleakest of situations. Even amid the imposed suffering, the prisoners holding a purpose survived and fared better than the prisoners who lost hope.

Frankl concluded from his experience, a prisoner's psychological reactions emanated from his freedom of choice even in the severest sufferings. In a prisoner's *freedom to* choose, suffering wasn't an unfortunate circumstance. Suffering gave them purpose in their choice. For example, Frankl points to a group of prisoners who willingly suffered the punishment of mass hunger rather than surrendering a fellow prisoner to certain death at the hands of the camp authorities. As a group, they chose suffering as a free and deliberate act. Their choice allowed them to see a future of hope, where life had meaning even if it didn't have meaning to the camp authorities.

The meaning of life is in every moment of living.

Meaning doesn't cease to exist in suffering or death, as in the case of the suffering prisoners. Suffering can carry deep and connected meaning. The prisoners' solidarity of purpose was rooted in their *freedom to* choose to suffer on behalf of the life of another.

BUILD FREEDOM TO MOMENTS

It can seem daunting to try and develop your *freedom to* choose muscle, your *agency*, in the middle of chaos. Building new ways of thinking is not as simple as deciding on a new line of thinking. Look to anyone setting a New Year's resolution. By February, 80 percent of people have abandoned their resolutions (Stahl 2021).

Is it easier to build your *freedom to* muscle with help. You need helicopter vision to see those *freedom to* building moments. Dr. Frankl provided the helicopter vision to his fellow prisoners. When you are on the road to building your *freedom to* muscle, you need helicopter vision.

When building your *freedom to* muscle, it's best to start small and celebrate even the most minor accomplishments because you are retraining your mind to think differently. Your actions may change as you train your mind to think differently. One small step in changing your agency will ripple to your personal life, work life, and social encounters with others. As you grow your *freedom to* capacity, you will affect the world, a lovely thought.

FREEDOM TO MOMENTS

Tools to build your *freedom to* muscle are not saying and believing you have agency. It's rather doing the work of agency. Here are a few *freedom to* building tools to slip into your toolbox.

PAUSE

When something miserable happens, pause before reacting. In this way, you break the cycle of reacting without thinking. Automatic emerges from habit. To create a new pattern, embed it in the already existing one. Instead of thinking negative thoughts, stop and pause.

Try this simple experiment. Notice how you feel and take stock of your mental disposition after reading the items below.

- This is going to be terrible.
- What awful news.
- It's horrible.
- This is going to be a significant setback.

Notice how you feel. Notice what sensations emerge for you and, if possible, jot them down. Continuing the experiment, read the following statements.

- What opportunity lies in there?
- What might this situation be teaching me?
- What's possible?
- What's hiding or missing to turn this around?

Again, as a simple experiment, notice how you feel and take stock of your mental disposition after reading the above. What is different for you? You may have noticed certain sensations associated with each set of statements. When I read the first statements, I noticed my belly gets unsettled. When I read the second set of statements, my mind goes into exploration mode, and my stomach settles. Pausing before reacting can help you avoid a negative or positive bias from what you experience because pausing can help you notice your sensations. When you respond, you can take those sensations into your decision-making process.

AND

When you disagree with a point of view, downcast Don shows up to tell you everything wrong with the world, or if you want to add to what he's saying, you can use the word *and.* The term *and* allows someone to turn horrible into an *and* moment. For example, take the following statements:

- This is terrible, and I wonder what opportunity lies in there.
- What awful news, and what might this situation be teaching me?
- It's horrible, and what's possible?
- This is a significant setback, and what's hidden or missing to turn this around?

People with agency don't overlook the awful. They recognize it, and they don't stop with horrible. The mistake many of us make is that we stop when we could be thinking of the next step, the one we can't see. Expand your thinking and expand your worldview to include your *and* moment.

YET

Another great *freedom to* tool for you is the word *yet.* I find myself using this word with my coaching clients, and as a trained coach, I find it helpful when my coach uses it on me. Here are a few examples of how to use it:

Instead of saying, "I haven't found the answer," say, "I haven't found the answer yet."

Instead of saying, "I don't know how to do that," say, "I don't know how to do that yet."

Instead of saying, "I haven't managed a 500-person department," say, "I haven't managed a 500-person department yet."

What disappointment in your life or others' lives can you turn into an *and* or a *yet* moment?

RISK IT ALL

Welcoming your second child is not how many would choose to begin a PhD journey. Working in the industry and traveling the globe while leading a senior group of engineers left me empty because I hadn't completed my dream of getting a higher academic degree. Knowing my aspirations, my husband, my biggest champion, encouraged me to pursue my dreams even when it meant braving the great unknown with two small kids.

Leaving a well-paying job and switching gears with little kids in tow fills me with nervous energy as a risky and frightening move even after doing it. I wanted new opportunities to apply my system expertise to biological challenges. With baby in hand, after acceptance at the Mayo Clinic, we worried about how to manage on a single income in a state where we knew no one. Resigning from my company meant my dreams were becoming a reality, and we were pivoting into risk and the unknown.

Dreams can be scary. Did I think of all the risks? Heck yeah. We moved to a state known to have snow eleven months out of the year from a place seeing snow maybe one-half day a year. I gave up my job, salary, health benefits, and employee benefits to move my growing family across the country to scrape by as a graduate school student.

I had no assurance that I would find a job after completing my education, training, and dissertation. I had no idea what school my kids would attend or how we would manage growing kids in a state where neither my husband nor I had a family or a support group. I didn't look or feel I had poise.

There is a fine line between excitement and nervous energy. I believe I had both at the time. In moving states with a growing family, I knew I couldn't do any of it alone. I had a husband believing in me and my talents. My husband moved us across the country for a nice hefty pay decrease, knowing we would make it work.

I found friends in Minnesota helping us adjust and adapt, and one became my best friend. We joined groups I still treasure to this day, even if we are no longer a part of those groups. I believe my ability to form, partake in groups, and seek companionship helped me build lifelong habits of surrounding myself with amazing peers and supportive people in my life.

I had a deep faith in a loving God, and my faith came to my aid on more than one occasion. Support alone couldn't account for why I sought out and grew comfortable with risk or at least with managing risk. Those are two different things. I am comfortable managing risk. I am less comfortable with risk itself.

Risk is a powerful poise tool. If you can't grow comfortable with risk, increase your comfort managing risk.

RISK PRODUCES EXPERIENCE WITH RISK

My parents, without formal schooling, had raised four children and put them through private school, three of whom had attended university, and all four managed to secure solid jobs. My parents had traveled the globe all with a by-the-hour, blue-collar job. My mother graduated from school in the third grade because her family needed her wages to feed the family after her father's murder.

I figured if my parents could raise four children in their circumstances, we could manage to move across the country on a similar single income. I didn't know how we would manage. I knew we would. I had no plan for how. I deeply believed in the goodness of the God of the universe. My faith would see us through the scariest part of my graduate career when a little over two years later, halfway through my training, my husband lost his job.

Risk, panic, and doubt—I felt them all. I learned to stay in the discomfort, remembering my parent's journey. One of my mentors, Dr. Lilach Lerman, came to our aid or perhaps I came to hers. She hired me to work in her lab as an image-processing assistant, a blessing in helping our family survive. I buckled down and worked on finishing my thesis, working in Lilach's lab and letting my husband handle the parenting and home. This period was one of the most harrowing moments in my career and one of the most blessed segments of our life, scraping by, eating plain food, and living a simple life.

Over the years, I've grown comfortable with risk in no small part due to my resiliency, agency, and my faith. We'll explore next how I've grown comfortable with risk and how you can grow comfortable with risk.

CHAPTER EIGHT

Pitfalls and Perfect Poise

You teach people how to treat you by what you allow, what you stop, and what you reinforce.

—T. GASKINS

Like power pitfalls, the poise landscape has its own set of challenges. Confusing poise with being rooted or having it all figured out is both a pitfall and a detour from perfecting your poise. More troubling is that habits can be your stumbling block to having poise. Habits can flood calm into a panic. Fear is another poise pitfall. We'll address each in exploring your perfect poise.

SELL-BY DATE

Do you notice foods have an expiration date? Soaps have expiration dates printed on them. Yep, soap past its prime won't get you as squeaky clean as a fresh bar of soap. I often ask clients for their sell-by date for their current role. Comfort can numb us to a position, a company, an organization, or a way of thinking that no longer challenges or serves us. There is nothing wrong with staying at a company, organization, or in a certain way of thinking. However, complacency can make you forget why your position, role, or way of thinking is as it is. Challenging your reasons for remaining in a role, organization, or way of thinking is a way to affirm, prune, or grow yourself.

As a colleague, Carolyn Stefanco, shared on LinkedIn (on September 27, 2022), "Understand your odds of success in a particular role and make decisions accordingly. After watching a truly awful CEO fire my colleagues one by one earlier in my career, I made the determination that I would get out before that happened to me. Taking action to avoid a career-diminishing experience is key when you are not set up for success."

Exploring your sell-by date is a way to set yourself up for success with poise. Having poise means you are willing to embrace growth and change. Here are a few principles to keep in mind for perfecting your poise.

PRINCIPLE ONE
Embrace growth.

Schari and I were walking down our employer's hallway one day when the lights flashed off. The fire alarm sounded. My eyes struggled to see through the dark all around us. I jumped and reached out for anything I could grab, panicking. Schari glided to a halt, took inventory of where we were, and walked us toward a door with deliberate purpose. I don't think Schari ever noticed I panicked. She was the model of composure.

Reflecting on this situation, I realized we weren't in total darkness. I could still see. My eyes needed time to adjust. My eyes required time to catch up with the sudden light change. I got my breathing under control, and seeing Schari's reaction helped me move with deliberate motion, a big lesson for me. I was away from the calm and composed demeanor I would have preferred.

Poor habits got me into this reactive state.

Habits formed over the years can become your biggest stumbling block to living a life with poise.

Beware of your thoughts, for they become words. Beware of your
words, for they become actions. Beware of your actions, for they become
habits. Beware of your habits, for they become your character. Beware of your
character, for it becomes your destiny.

—FRANK OUTLAW

PRINCIPLE TWO
Identify your vision in explicit detail.

Identifying your vision may entail looking back.

Thinking back on the moment of darkness, I wanted to remain calm because if I could remain calm, I knew I could be a leader helping others discover calm. Being a calm leader in any situation is what I wanted to embody. I would be leading with a deliberate purpose. I would conduct myself and others steadily through the dark. I would be breathing steadily and pausing before reacting. I would assess the situation, determine the best path forward with the persons in my company, and then act. This was my vision. I found small ways to make this vision a reality.

Most of all, I wanted honesty and collaboration in my leadership, leading to the following principle.

PRINCIPLE THREE
Assess your current starting point.

Being honest meant I had to name what I felt. I felt fear in the dark. Once I named it, I stripped fear of its power. I was also able to pinpoint what I wanted.

In seeing my starting point with clarity, I could also see what the future looked like for me. I could see the difference between my end goal and my starting point. I also took inventory of the stuff I possessed, my unique resources.

These resources are always with me: I can carry heavy loads or what to others seem like heavy loads, metaphorically speaking. I am spiritual. Spiritual doesn't necessarily mean religious, although I am religious too. I feel most at ease when leading or helping others lean into their leadership. These are my resources, my superpowers. What resources do you have at your starting point?

Resources are something different from your strengths. Several assessments can highlight your strengths or get you started discovering your strengths. Your resources are your unique gifts, many of which you aren't even aware you possess. I didn't know I could carry heavy loads, nor did I know they were heavy. A superpower can go unnoticed until others point it out.

I started my graduate school career with kids in tow. While my fellow students were studying, working in their labs, and thinking about weekend parties, I was doing most of the same things, plus raising a couple of kids as my husband was gone most of the week. I grew accustomed to carrying heavier loads than my peers. When my husband lost his job, I shifted from a student finishing my thesis and taking care of the kids to working full-time between writing, researching, and doing my experiments. I stretched.

In stretching, I discovered how to use eight highway lanes for myself, even though we lived in a city with at most two lanes.

- Kids and family, lane one.
- Working the job, lane two.
- Finishing the thesis, lane three.
- Exercise and recharging, lane four.
- Next job and future, lane five.
- New skills, lane six.
- Volunteering, lane seven.
- Resting and vacation, lane eight.
- Prayer, emergency lane.

Out of necessity, I learned how to use each lane. My colleagues and friends wondered how I did everything in the same week they had. I told them I had 168 hours and navigated eight lanes or more with help. Over the years, the lanes have changed. I repurposed one of the lanes for this book. I have grown accustomed to navigating eight lanes (or more) in my life. What I didn't know was that others didn't have this eight-lane highway resource I had. This was my blind spot. I can help my clients use eight lanes or more in their lives. If my eight lanes help you, take it. Use it.

Beep. Beep.

If you don't know what resources or superpowers you possess, I invite you to explore this topic with a coach, a thought partner, or someone trained to help you identify your unique resources. Here is an exercise I use with my clients. The exercise may help you discover your amazing superpowers:

How to find your superpowers:

- Recall a time when you were proud of something you did or helped orchestrate. (I got my PhD.)
- What about this stands out to you? (What stands out is that I finished this while working and having a family, without abundant resources like money, family support, or time.)
- What amazes others about you? Ask them. (My colleagues are amazed at how much I can do, at what I can accomplish, at how I look at the world, and at my positivity.)
- Bring all your discoveries back together. Noodle over it. Act it. Journal. Pray. Reflect with your coach on your data and draw a few conclusions. (I can carry heavy loads.)

- Take it back to your coach, friends, and colleagues, and discuss it with them. "Hey, I think my superpower is_____. What do you think?" They may ask you questions, nod their heads profusely, saying, "Oh, my gosh. Yes!" or give you feedback, "Actually, I think it's more you _____." (When I shared with my friends my observations, I got overwhelming feedback, "Yes!")
- Whatever the feedback, say, "Thank you. I appreciate you telling me."
- Noodle on it and repeat this exercise often.

We all have superpowers. It would be a shame to let yours go unnoticed or unrecognized because you didn't take the time to discover them.

PRINCIPLE FOUR
You have options.

Identify potential options to get you to your vision.

I wanted calm instead of panic when I was in the dark. Wishing for serenity didn't work. I needed new behaviors, requiring me to build those behaviors. In facing the unknown, I recognized that my shoulders would tense. I held my breath, panic ensued, and my stomach got queasy. I looked for these sensations. I became the tense shoulder police and dispatched an all-points bulletin for when my shoulders tensed. When I located my suspect, I relaxed my shoulders and breathed, telling myself how calm I was.

I found a few options and used my superpowers.

Breathing and prayer were a big part of my path to calm. My clients tell me I have a calm, supportive, and challenging style. Even before I discovered my calm in the middle of a dark storm, my friends would tell me I had a calming voice. I lacked the calm demeanor in uncertainty to go along with my calm voice. Knowing my superpower is that I can carry heavy loads means I can remind myself in the uncertainty of my inner strength. Other superpowers, the things unique and easy for me to do, include spirituality. I developed a prayer habit. When I let prayer slip away, my inner calm fades. My prayer involves a relationship with someone bigger than me. When my relationship is good, everything becomes manageable. I won't say easy. If you are looking for easy, you'll find it in the presence section.

PRACTICE WITH YOUR OPTIONS

Habits don't appear out of thin air, even bad ones. We form habits from practiced behavior. Practice the behavior, and it becomes a habit (Fogg 2019; Clear 2018). Practice makes permanent. Part of the practice is experimenting with what works, throwing out what doesn't, and keeping what works. Forming a habit is a messy process.

REJOICE AND CELEBRATE

A celebration doesn't mean chocolate cake. A smile, a high five, or a pat on your back can all suffice for a small celebration as you develop your new messy habit. I may not change my body's initial reaction to pitch-black overnight. I can change how I respond to it. I have changed how I react to this fear.

By practicing these principles, working with your options, and celebrating your new behaviors, you can progress in perfecting your poise and growing comfortable with your discomfort.

PERFECT POISE

The essence of being human is that one does not seek perfection.
—GEORGE ORWELL

Perfect poise is dancing and allowing a stranger to lead you to a tune you don't know. Poise trusts you can dance and you'll figure it out on the dance floor. The truth of the matter is that perfect poise isn't perfect.

TRUST

I sing in the choir. In reality, I screech, but sure, let's say I sing. When I would get a new piece to sing, I would try to read the notes and the words while singing and watching for direction from our choir director, Ms. Freda. My glasses being split prescription change my clarity depending on where I gaze. What ended up happening was that I would lose my place and sing a mixture of words (not necessarily the right ones) with the wrong notes or wrong emphasis. I rested when I should have been singing and crescendoed when I shouldn't have.

At one point, I got frustrated and changed tactics. I read the lyrics, kept my eyes on Ms. Freda, and trusted my voice would do as she conducted. One would not describe my singing as pitch-perfect or in tune. However, I had found perfect poise.

FROM FEAR TO POISE

Clara told me the story of a colleague.

"He left the company a couple of years ago for another role, and now he's returned two levels above where he was when he left," Clara said.

"When he returned," she continued, "he had more confidence, had outside knowledge he gained from working in a different company, acquired new skills from his company, brought competitive knowledge and how others do things differently. He took a big risk leaving the company. It paid off."

"Clara, what are you thinking?" I said.

"Well, when I see it all together, he took a risk. It was a calculated risk. Our company didn't have many opportunities back then. He moved out to a similar company in a higher role, and he didn't know anybody there. Now he does. He stayed for a couple of years, and we had a few new openings. I didn't feel I could apply for those roles because it would have been two-level jumps. There still isn't anything here for me, and he now has a bigger network of peers. I'm ready to look around for my next step," said Clara.

When Clara saw these interweaved risks and benefits, she got comfortable with the thought of taking a calculated risk. Clara found herself ready to play with calculated risk, one step at a time.

IT'S NOT A MASTERPIECE

A duck gliding in a pond looks serene. Underwater, they paddle like mad. Poise. My clients often believe that what they feel inside signals they don't have poise. They want to feel inside like they appear on the outside. I want my family to dispense with the drama. I'm not going to get my wish. I can take my discomfort and let it paddle with furious speed while I stay calm and serene as the unsupervised kid launches the remote control at the clock or the dog again. We can remain unmoved while emotions and experiences unfold within us or at us.

When John Watson asked Sherlock to be his best man, Sherlock shared all the excitement, joy, sorrows, anticipation, stress, worries, and joy he felt with John. However, when Sherlock recounts the story to the wedding reception audience, he shares, "It later transpired I had said none of this out loud" (McCarthy 2014).

Sherlock stood in silent stillness as all these emotions coursed through his body, having what he thought was a conversation with the groom. My son does the same thing. When anything monumental happens, for example, we bring home a baby sister from the hospital to meet her brother, or we want to watch a movie saga out of chronological order, my son will stand in silent stillness.

His papa calls it, "Apples, apples, apples, everywhere," to let us know our son is collecting imaginary apples from his tipped-over apple cart. His world has shifted, and his apple cart spilled everywhere. He's silent and collecting apples to put them back in his newly moved cart.

This is perfect poise. Perfect poise can feel like apples everywhere no one sees, long conversations spoken to no one in particular, paddling like a maniac in one area of your life to glide smoothly in another. Perfect poise does not feel perfect. If you're waiting for perfection, you'll be waiting for a long time. Perfect poise is uncomfortable. Perhaps one day, you will grow comfortable with the discomfort, and when you do, it'll be time to level up your poise factor.

RISK
Time to pony up and talk risk. The way to grow comfortable with risk is to experiment with it in small doses and in safe situations. Safe doesn't mean risk-free.

In my choir situation, I sing off-key. I'm singing the wrong words, notes, or both. Often, I do a solo. I don't do this on purpose. It is an accident because I should have been singing with the choir. Whoops.

When we sing in unison and on pitch, the sound is magical. A stray note here or there won't end the service. The congregation is generous and forgiving. I've heard their singing. The worst outcome is that I might be embarrassed and get a reproachful look, and the best to happen is magic. Steadying myself for looks, magic, or somewhere in between made me comfortable taking the risk to sing, even when I'm off-key. Another way to grow your risk tolerance is to look risk straight in the eye.

As I grew my coaching practice, I got into the habit of doing something to scare, terrify, or thrill me.

I cringed whenever I thought about recording and listening to my coaching conversations. In my discomfort, I overlooked a significant opportunity. When I confronted my discomfort, I discovered that listening with curiosity opened a vast opportunity for improving my coaching skills. My coaching skills grew by leaps and bounds as I listened to my coaching conversations with a mentor or supervisor coach.

What I used to see as uncomfortable and *risky* is something I don't even notice anymore. Here are a few things I did to build my risk muscle, in case you want to start growing yours:

- I asked myself, "What scary thing are you going to do today?"
- I questioned myself, "What thrilling thing can you do today?"
- I pondered, "What would you do without consequences?"
- I tallied these responses, and I started doing the legal ones, such as:
  - Posted on social media.
  - Commented on others' social media accounts.
  - Talked to strangers. (I'm not a friendly, chatty person by nature.)
  - I introduced myself to someone I didn't know.
  - Joined a club.

- Volunteered to serve on a board of directors.
- Started a blog.
- Got a website.
- Started a podcast.
- Published a newsletter.
- Introduced colleagues to sponsors.
- Spoke at a national meeting.
- Spoke on a TEDx stage.
- I wrote down my thoughts. (Be careful what you do. This last one turned into a book.)

Every day became a new day of asking myself, what exciting thing will I do today? How will I make myself uncomfortable today? I try to aim for at least one way to be uncomfortable every day. This single technique has made me more of a risk-taker and more outgoing. What scared me before doesn't anymore. Perhaps building your risk muscle can do the same for you.

As you explore and play with your risk tolerance, you may discover power, weaving in with your poise. Don't panic. This is a good sign.

What if you are the other persuasion, someone comfortable with risk? Then the opposite is also true. Your path to excel in poise may lie in your ability to stay when you're itching to entertain risk. You may be missing critical data in your haste and comfort with risk.

PRESENCE

CHAPTER NINE

Presence

———

Give a girl the right shoes, and she can conquer the world.
—BETTE MIDLER

Mya radiated a commanding presence, poised to take on a new business opportunity. She told me, "I built up a new business from scratch and gave it to another leader a few years ago. Since then, it's grown to over 500 persons strong. They have asked me to come back to the business." She faltered, shoulders sinking, telling me, "You see, the current business leader has allowed competitiveness to destroy the culture. There is a lot of infighting among his leaders, destroying the team atmosphere. This is the way he operates. Well, company leadership has called *me* to come back to the business to rescue the department. It would mean two levels of promotion for me. They are working on the promotion application. My problem is that I don't manage departments. I can't do what he does," she said.

"Mya, what do you do that no one else can do?" I said.

"Easy. I build businesses from nothing. I pull in the right experts. I get the business going, make it successful and hand it off to someone else. Then I build again. This is different. He [the current leader] is a well-known figure in the tech community. I don't have his technical expertise. I don't know the first thing about running his business or having his following. He gets engagements in the thousands right away when he posts on social media. Others pick it up and repost it. He has a massive following on social media. I worry about filling his shoes," Mya said, sighing.

"And he couldn't lead a profitable business and build a healthy team atmosphere," I summarized.

"Well, running a business is no small task, but I worry I can't fill his shoes. I wouldn't know what to post on social media. He posts on LinkedIn, and it gets recognized, recirculated, and thousands of people engage with him. I don't have his knowledge. I don't know how I'm going to fill his shoes. He's got the admiration of the industry. Those are shoes I don't know how to step into. Maybe I should hire a social media consultant. What do you think?" Mya said, peering at me.

What had happened to the confident, present leader from earlier? She was wrestling with someone else's stinky shoes, wanting to fit into them, and wanted my advice for her social media hiring practices. Presence, the quality living within Mya, vanished (Blake 2019).

PRESENCE

Presence inspires confidence in others. It's hard to inspire confidence if you don't have it yourself. If presence vanishes in a moment, we can recover it in a moment, something we'll do together. Presence refers to your appearance and bearing, a dignified approach or personality, and an invisible spirit felt by others.

Confidence is having the air of certainty or a feeling of consciousness of your faith or beliefs to act appropriately regardless of circumstance. I've had clients with varying degrees of confidence.

A lack of confidence prevents you from seeing the broader picture and makes you doubt yourself. When a lack of confidence strikes, a narrow vision is the sneaky culprit. Mya needed a vision reset. Her presence self-assessment could provide clear clues to what was getting in her way.

CONFIDENCE

If you've helped a friend in need, you have had confidence. When you attend to your friend, you're probably not concerned about yourself. Your vision is outward, focused on another. You might lack the expanded capacity to act with confidence in other contexts, but you likely have the skill of confidence.

However, let's say you can't act with confidence. Let's assume you have not known or worked with confidence once in your life. Confidence is being certain and having faith, and believing in yourself. Suppose you can say honestly that you have not felt confident in your life. If not, a single thing exists you have acted upon with certainty, then you are the rare breed embodying confidence in lacking confidence. Hold on to the feeling. This is what confidence feels like for you. You have confidence and are haggling over the price you want to pay to have confidence.

Given you have confidence in at least one area of your life, we can do the work of expanding your capacity to other areas of your life. Your presence will follow.

PRESENCE ASSESSMENT
Find a quiet space to ponder your assessment. You will finish the evaluation quicker if you turn off all distractions. Take a few deep breaths, and don't worry about checking your phone or your email. Take your time in completing this entire section.

THINKING BACK TO WHEN YOU WEREN'T COMMANDING YOUR PRESENCE, WHAT WAS GOING ON FOR YOU?
Consider a challenge where you struggle to be present the way you want. This can be a situation where you want to inspire confidence in others or yourself. A situation or a painful memory may arise, not representing your best self. This may be a situation haunting you or replaying in your memory, wishing the situation would have turned out differently.

WHEN IMAGINING YOURSELF LACKING PRESENCE, WHAT WORDS COME TO MIND?
Words can capture moments like photos capture memories. What are some of the words coming to mind for you? Ample, small, light, airy, off-balance, out of tune, shattered?

WHAT MOVEMENTS, IF ANY, SIGNAL YOU ARE NOT PRESENT WITH CONFIDENCE?

When you lack presence or confidence, you may recognize motion or no motion. Jot down what comes to mind for you.

WHAT SHAPE DOES YOUR LACK OF PRESENCE HAVE?

Shapes are funny things. Our body is a shape. Our bodies can make different shapes. What shapes, if any, come to mind when pondering this moment when you aren't present the way you want to be?

WHAT SENSATIONS DOES A LACK OF PRESENCE EVOKE, IF ANY?

Sensations are all around you, within you, and you can perceive them outside of you. What trends do you perceive connected to your lack of presence?

DESCRIBE ONE OR TWO OF THOSE SENSATIONS MORE.

Go deeper with one or two of the stronger sensations. Describe them in simple terms.

OF THE STRONGER SENSATIONS, WHERE IS ITS SOURCE OF ORIGIN?

Origin stories, heroes, and villains—all have origin stories. Where does your lack of presence or lack of confidence originate?

WHAT ARE YOUR MANNERISMS AND BEHAVIORS WHEN YOU LACK PRESENCE?

Manners and behaviors come from you. You may be fidgety, talkative, darting, or full of gestures.

WHAT DOES A LACK OF PRESENCE FEEL LIKE TO YOU?

Summarize the findings. Without judgment, capture what you've discovered, similar to how you'd alert your Twitter followers that you found a new continent. Your followers can use your information when looking for the new continent based on your description, or you can use this description to increase your awareness when your presence starts to fade.

PRESENCE

Switching into your presence space, take a moment to consider how presence feels in your person. You may recall a moment from your recent or distant past where you showed up with presence, filled with confidence.

OF WHAT DOES YOUR PRESENCE REMIND YOU?

Various moments, ideas, persons, places, or things can spring to mind. Please take a moment to jot them down.

WHAT IS HAPPENING DIFFERENTLY FROM BEFORE?

A whole different perception may arise when you are present. It may have color, shape, space, sounds, or flavors. What are they?

WHAT COLOR IS YOUR PRESENCE?

Red, white, gold, sparkles, rainbows, gray, yellow, midnight sky—possibilities are endless. What are yours?

WHAT SHAPE DOES YOUR PRESENCE HAVE, IF ANY?

Your presence may have a shape. It may not.

HOW DO YOU KNOW YOUR PRESENT, CONFIDENT SELF SHOWS UP FOR YOU?

What signals you are present or confident? Be a scientist and discover the tell-tale signs signaling you are confident and present.

WHERE DO YOU FEEL YOUR PRESENCE EMERGING IN YOUR BODY, MIND, OR SPIRIT?

We are getting closer to discovering where your presence calls home. Where can you feel it?

DESCRIBE YOUR PRESENT CONFIDENT SELF.

Does your presence have a motion? If so, up, down, right, left, around, or under? Is it light, heavy, big, or small?

WHERE IS YOUR PRESENT CONFIDENT SELF, CENTERED?

Earthquakes have epicenters. Your presence has a center. Where is the center?

SUMMARIZE YOUR FINDINGS.

Like a scientist noting the growth of plants in the garden, review your notes and make a summary for yourself. You make new neural connections when writing these out. Skip this step at your loss.

These are your presence biomarkers. These distinguishing features (posture, feelings, center, motion, and sensations) make up your presence. You can jot these down on your presence recipe card.

Considering your presence, what do you now know about showing up with presence?

PRESENCE

Posture_____
Feels Like_____
Center_____
Motion_____
Sensation_____

Figure 1. Presence biomarker recipe card.

MYA

Remember Mya? She wanted my advice on hiring a social media consultant. I have no qualifications for advising for or against a social media consultant. I was sure she knew the answer to the question she hadn't asked. She had asked me if she should hire a social media consultant. Here is how I responded.

"It seems knowing the answer to your question is important to you," I said to Mya.

"Yes, and why I asked you," she said.

"If you did know the answer to your question, Mya, what would be different for you?" I said.

"I guess I wouldn't be questioning myself. I would be moving forward." Her shoulders straightened while her voice deepened.

"What else, Mya?"

"I wouldn't doubt myself because when I'm sure of myself, it's like I'm walking on air. I ask for outside advice but from the point of curiosity, not from wanting to do the advice given. See, when I asked you what I should do, it was like looking for someone else's answer. Even when I don't know my answer but am sure of myself, I look at things from all angles. Not what I'm doing here. I wanted your angle, but when I think about it, your view is only one angle."

"Mya, when you know, it seems you don't doubt yourself. You're looking from all angles, walking on air, your shoulders straight, your voice seems to deepen, and your questions come from curiosity. What did I miss?"

"I didn't consider it the way you said," said Mya, with a far-off look.

"What do you know now, Mya?"

"It's funny you ask because I was thinking, why am I trying to fit into his stinky ol' shoes?"

"Survey says?" I wondered.

"It's not even about the social media consultant. I was really wrestling with not feeling like I belonged in this role."

"It seems like you found something out about yourself."

"I thought I needed a PhD to run the department. I was telling myself I didn't deserve the role."

"Hmmm. Didn't deserve the role."

"That's ridiculous. They would be lucky to have me."

"And your social media consultant?"

"Maybe I need one, but not because it'll make me fit into the role." She paused and smiled. She said, "It'll be because I want one. I don't need anyone else's shoes. Mine fit me fine."

Your presence may be friendly, breathing steady, and staying on topic, or your presence might feel, look and be a pair of high-heeled shoes or boots. Whatever presence means for you, when you find it, no one else can take it from you because it is custom fit and tailored for you.

PRESENCE TOOLS AND TECHNIQUES

With a better understanding of your presence biomarkers, you can practice working with your biomarkers to show up with your sense of presence. Strengthening your presence will require reexamining laser speaking. Since emotions can derail presence, we'll examine emotions next with presence tools and techniques.

CHAPTER TEN

Presence Tools

———

Walking is nothing more than falling and catching yourself each time you take a step.

—YANG WANG

I would have been friends with Heidi in a heartbeat. Being upbeat, optimistic, and friendly made her a fun companion. I was surprised to learn more about Heidi when I asked, "Where are we going today, Heidi?"

"I'm in my new job, and I must give a presentation to my group. I've done this many times. I don't know this group. I'm new. I'm afraid," she said.

"What exactly is happening when you are afraid?" I said.

"It's happened before when I must give direct feedback or if I'm in meetings and I think my opinion will clash with someone else's. I don't know anyone in my new place. I'm not looking forward to this presentation because I can talk too long when I'm nervous, and my message gets confusing. I'm scared of making a bad impression," she said.

Have you been in a similar situation?

Aside from equipping Heidi with her presence recipe, we outfitted her with fear-fighting tactics and tools.

EMOTIONS

Personality, beliefs, thoughts, and emotions, positive or negative, you and other humans have and express them. Part of life is experiencing the whir of emotions, nervous energy, laughter, fear, anger, disgust, and enjoyment, to name a few. Emotions can be overwhelming, make you feel out of control, cause stress, or be an emotional roller coaster with twists and turns.

Emotions, instinctive or intuitive feelings, are energy. Emotions communicate essential knowledge. However, the communication is similar to a two-year-old lacking full command of spoken language. Emotions speak through sensations in your body. I find our gut adult reaction is to ignore or bury them when we should instead learn how to ride the wave of emotions. You can observe or ignore your emotions, attempting to bury them. Ignoring emotions turns into trying to control a two-year-old temper tantrum, a hot, wriggling mess. A lot of good holding your emotions will do you when you're irritated and about to have an outburst in front of your staff or well up with tears, an experience Angela had.

ANGELA'S TEARS

Angela and I met to get clarity for her future career. She was frustrated with her clinical and research duties at the hospital. She was pondering leaving it all and finding a new job outside medicine. Her calendar had little to no availability, despite having "protected time" to "keep up her research work." She struggled to fit any research work into her week. Angela was "in more meetings than I ever thought was possible," she told me. She had "less and less time to complete clinical duties, let alone do any research."

During a contentious meeting with her department chair, they asked her to expand her responsibilities. She told me, "I was struggling to hold a conversation. I was barely speaking to him and broke down in tears at one point. I felt mortified and humiliated. I want to learn how to handle my emotions to avoid this happening again."

"Angela, you're not alone in this. I've been there too. What was going on before you broke down in tears?" I said.

She said, "He told me I'd have to pick up another rotation. I felt my throat get hot. My throat tightened."

"What might your hot tightening throat signify?"

"My body tells me not to speak. I was fighting it. I forced myself to speak, and I broke down into tears."

Emotions carry energy. When you stop to examine energy, profound and powerful information can emerge. You can take the information you discover and choose what you want to do with it.

Options. You always have options.

DEALING WITH EMOTIONS

When emotions arise, you can have a game plan you can use. It is simple:

- Notice
- Be open
- Be gentle

You don't have to do anything with your emotions. The emotions themselves aren't dangerous.

Notice and be open to the insight emotions carry. Don't judge yourself or say anything harsh. Be gentle. This applies whether you are experiencing the feelings or you are receiving the emotions. The exception is never to tolerate violence, regardless of if the violence is from a two-year-old temper tantrum or a forty-two-year-old tantrum. We'll talk about the two-year-old in later chapters. If there is violence, seek safety.

The next step after noticing the emotion is to explore your options. You always have options. You may not appreciate your options. However, you have them. My favorite is riding the wave. I may stay with cravings when I crave sweet treats, knowing my craving is a wave. Waves have peaks and valleys. When I am feeling an urge, I examine where I am in the wave, peaking or subsiding. If I stay with my sensations instead of sinking under the craving wave, I know the craving will valley. Riding the wave means choosing to stay with whatever you are experiencing. I can choose to give in to the craving. Either way, I've made a powerful choice of being present.

Here are a few other options for you:

- Breathe and experience the emotion with fullness appreciating the wave. Ride the wave.
- Voice your feelings. Either aloud or internally. "I'm noticing anger is present." Voicing what you feel may sound silly. Voicing is empowering. Your Wernicke's area, located in the superior temporal gyrus of your left cerebral hemisphere, typically right behind your ear, is where you comprehend speech. Your Broca's area is in the front of your left cerebral hemisphere, where your ideas and thoughts turn into spoken words. When you voice your opinions and thoughts, you engage various parts of your brain, from Broca's area to the motor cortex to Wernicke's area, giving you more neural connections than a simple thought (Boron 2005).
- If you are being judgmental and thinking, *I should, I must, I ought to, I need to*, or any other judgment, then swap your *should* to *I choose to* or *I choose not to*, as a way to empower yourself to be present.
- Play it out. Use your imagination and give voice to your imagination. For example, you could say, "I'm angry. I want to scream. I'm going to look strange and awkward in the hotel lobby, yelling like a banshee." You'll get to ridiculous, funny, or outlandish quickly.

- Remove yourself from the situation. Think to yourself, *Lizette is getting tough feedback; let me be a secretary right now and make sure I catch it to review it with her later.*
- Look at your situation from a different angle. You might say, "One day, I will be one of these poor people in the pews next to a mother with a fussy child, and when it's my turn, I will have compassion for them. They are doing the best they can."
- Find a working phrase for you and express it. For example, you could say, "I am a full human with a variety of emotions," or "Emotions are energy," "This sucks," or "This feeling will pass," or "The stars shine even when I can't see them."
- Reroute the energy and get active. Go for a walk, do push-ups, or jog in place.
- Do nothing except pause. A pause may seem like an eternity. Adding three, five, or ten seconds to your pause can mean the difference between the peak of an emotional crest and tipping to the other manageable side, plus silence primes your audience to listen to you. Your next few words will be heavier in your audience's comprehension, especially if the next word is "No." If your reply isn't a "Heck yeah," then consider saying "No," preceded and followed by silence.

The next step is my favorite step of all, capturing the essence of working with emotions in a fun way. Play around with your options. The play is critical because no solid winning technique will work for all. You might have a method working well for you. If you find a working option, great. Remember, a working option is not the expectation. Play is. The point is to play around and find an option suitable for you.

When dealing with emotions, remember:

Notice—be open to options—be gentle and play.

PRESENCE IN COMMUNICATIONS

I promised we'd revisit laser speaking after exploring your confidence because one of the impediments to laser speaking is a lack of confidence. Heidi pointed out her lack of confidence in being in a new situation and having to give a presentation to an audience where she didn't have friends or know people well. We'll revisit laser communication using Heidi's dilemma.

HEIDI

I asked Heidi more about when she had felt present and confident in the past when presenting or talking to others, and this is what she said:

"I have friends around me, people I know and trust. My breathing is steady. I stay on topic and am not worried about what I'm saying because I'm talking to my friends and people I know."

For her to laser speak, she needed:

- friends around her
- knowing her audience
- steady breathing
- to stay on topic

Heidi chose to imagine she had a room full of friends. She wanted to imagine she had worked with this team for years, and they knew and treasured each other. Heidi tried to remind herself to breathe and be present with her friends. Heidi also thought she'd remind herself to stay on topic with her friends. Heidi permitted herself to experiment with what might work well for her.

Heidi had room to play and explore in her new settings. This gave her a unique perspective on having fun with exploring her present and confident self. Instead of being nervous and afraid of new situations, she looked forward to them because she could imagine she knew her audience and they were already good friends.

Heidi shared with me, "Lizette, I gave a great talk. I did what we practiced, and I had fun. There was a moment when I felt nervous and reminded myself of what we did last time. It worked."

ENLISTING HELP

Joseph, my good friend, has a housekeeper and a cook. I used to get jealous that his employer provided housekeeping services to him. I'd think, *If I had a cleaner and a cook, I could save time. Not fair!* I would steam in my irritation until I learned to be grateful for him having help. I found an opportunity in gratitude.

Against my husband's wishes, I hired a cleaner and purchased a food prep service. The food prep service has taught us other ways to prepare food. My husband learned how to cook excellent healthy meals from the food prep investment. We've expanded our culinary capabilities and gained time. The housekeeper has helped me declutter my house. When I have a clean desk, I can think easier. When the housekeeper finishes cleaning, I always find a few things I can clear or throw out. I lost money and gained time. Money is renewable. Time is not.

Enlisting help isn't a weakness. Enlisting help is a weakness leaving you. Embrace help.

Henry was similar to my client Edmund from chapter 4. Henry is the company president, finding himself working at all hours, being the chief people officer, creating and vetting strategy for the business, assisting his employees and his leaders with their problems, and worrying about how he will make it all work. When Henry outlined his typical day for me, I poked him, "Henry, who's doing the work only you can do?"

We all have activities we can do, are good at doing, and aren't good at doing. When we are doing the activities others can do, who is doing what only you can do?

Prioritize the activities only you can do. No one else can do it for you.

ENLISTING HELP FROM LEADERSHIP TEAMS

Anne is a leader with an executive leadership team. An executive leadership team helps her make decisions and helps carry a load of leadership and decision-making, providing her guidance and wisdom. Any good leadership team should do these things. You don't have to be an executive leader to have a leadership team. I introduce leadership teams to my clients. I coach several leadership teams for various professionals, from emerging leaders to established and elite leaders, because I find leadership teams a powerful career-enhancing resource.

Teams are more productive when their skills are complementary. Teams also have a stronger basis from which to solve tricky problems (Wakefield 2013). The trick for successful high-performing leadership teams at work or as a career resource is to have a sound structure with a compelling purpose and a good supporting context, enabling trust, vulnerability, and a strong group dynamic to emerge, not an accident (Clutterbuck 2019). Rarely does a high-performing team occur without the investment of coaching.

A small number of diverse members compose a professional leadership team. Their resources together in new combinations, tackle common challenges and obstacles for all on the leadership team. Group coaching is a type of career leadership team. Chief, a private network focused on connecting and supporting women executives, supports their women executives through peer core groups, a particular type of group coaching aimed at executive women leaders (Chief 2019).

Tiger21 is an exclusive group coaching club for high-networth individuals, where membership begins for members having over $20 million in investable assets (Sonnenfeldt 2022). From group coaching serving various individual needs to Chief, helping elite women leaders to Tiger21 serving ultra-high-net-worth individuals, there is a leadership team awaiting you. The cost of coaching can drive people away. Group coaching is a sustainable and affordable option worth exploring.

If you don't want to seek out a leadership team, you can put together your leadership team. Yours might include your neighbor, colleague, friend, church volunteer, pastor, and perhaps someone you befriended on LinkedIn. You can assemble your leadership team and organizational leadership team meetings with the promise of fellowship, treats, or to help you with the following agenda:

- Welcome the team and recap the rules. I provide a few examples of how to do this.
  - Welcome and introductions.
    - "Welcome. Thanks for joining. Here is what I am looking for from my Leadership team today. I am struggling with whether I should seek a new job."
    - List your specific needs instead if you aren't seeking a new job.
  - "Ask me questions. I don't need your solutions. I need to find my own, and I need your help."
  - "Be curious with your questions."
  - "If you have something to share from your experience, I welcome hearing it."
  - "We'll use thirty minutes and then have refreshments. Who can lead us today to keep us on time?"
- Encourage questions and answer questions honestly.
- At the end of the allotted time, recap what you have learned with your team.
- Thank your team.

Using this framework, you can get to know your leadership team better, and others may bring topics to the team. You can start with one to two people and grow your team over time.

You are modeling leadership when you ask and show others how to help. Leadership gives first and receives second.

INTERNAL LEADERSHIP TEAMS

Another type of leadership team resource is an internal leadership team. Maddie learned this model from our coaching. Her first leadership team was a group of inner voices, her voice of doubt, her voice of confidence, her voice of approval, her voice of financial analyst, and her voice of bully.

"Maddie, when you receive the nomination and serve as a leader, your leadership team is there to support and challenge you. We all have leadership teams living within us. For your internal leadership team, you get to nominate the voices you want on your team and when you want them to contribute. If your voice of doubt is hogging the floor, as team leader, you get to tell doubt to take a seat because you want to hear from a quiet one, confidence, for example. You get to pick. What do you think?" I asked.

"It sounds interesting. This voice of financial analyst I keep having telling me to recheck the numbers is on my team? I'm not sure how to start," she said.

"What other entities have we identified, whether characters or voices?" I said.

"There's doubt, always nagging me. The bully told me how I did things wrong or it was wrong. The analyst has me checking and rechecking. There is also another, quiet voice of confidence and the questioning voice, in a good way, asking me the question I hadn't thought of and not causing me to doubt myself," she said.

You are the leader of your team, and you get to staff your team however you see fit. In partnering with a coach or a thought partner, you can staff your leadership team with characters or personalities playing a role in your life or you want to play a role in your life. You may even choose to have power, poise, and presence characters on your leadership team.

The purpose of any leadership team (in real life or imagination) is to challenge, support, celebrate, and advocate for you.

Using your presence biomarkers, getting help, working with a team, and playing with your options can work for you, too, or fail. Failure is what we tackle next for your perfect presence.

CHAPTER ELEVEN

Pitfalls and Perfect Presence

———

Do not be afraid to break out of the comfortable and routine modes of living.

—POPE JOHN PAUL II

Audrey, the business leader for a global corporation, prepared the business innovation plan for the leadership team review. During the presentation, someone asked her: "Share what you have on the market activation plan for this year's products." Her business innovation plan hadn't gotten approval, and the market activation plan for the products belonged to another leader. The market activation plan and the business innovation plan had in common the word plan. However, different organizational members ran both.

Audrey told me, "I completely unraveled. I wasn't expecting to present someone else's plan. I was trying to think what to say as they sat there looking at me for answers I didn't have. I was embarrassed that I couldn't even answer questions when *I knew* the answers. My boss had to step in and salvage the rest of the meeting. Lizette, what do I do so I don't crumble? I don't want this to happen again," said Audrey through tears.

If your confidence wavers, similar to Audrey's, you are not alone. The tools in this chapter will encourage you to broaden your vision. When your vision is too narrow, your presence and confidence can crumble. Once confidence crumbles, your presence has no foundation.

Perfect presence doesn't have everything together and knows all the answers.

Knowing all the answers isn't presence. Knowing all the answers is being a dictionary.

Presence is open to not knowing all the answers and still having confidence in yourself. Presence has nothing to do with anyone else except you, where we start.

NOT KNOWING

One of the biggest confidence derailers is admitting, "I don't know," or seeing challenges as threats to our egos rather than an opportunity to learn (Grant 2021). When going through my PhD training, one of the learning opportunities happened when the "evil thesis committee" would challenge the trainee, me, or another unfortunate fellow in public no less. It's uncomfortable to stand in front of any audience and be challenged by respected professors on a topic where you are supposedly the expert. They asked me many questions when

I did not know the answers. This is a familiar ritual. Get the fellow to admit they don't know.

One of this ritual's objectives is to lead the trainee to admit they don't know something in public, a vulnerable space for a burgeoning expert and someone with years of schooling, research, and experience in their résumé. Not knowing and admitting you don't know in public can be defeating, making you feel like a fraud and oddly liberating for others.

Years of training, study, and forcibly realizing you don't know can make you feel you don't belong. The truth is the exact opposite. The point of these public exercises of getting the trainee to realize what they don't know isn't humiliation hazing. Instead, these events open the trainee to the inquiry process.

If you can't admit what you don't know, you can't start the inquiry process. The inquiry process can't begin until you realize you don't know.

You aren't meant to know it all. A framework for thinking and processing information gives you organization for your thoughts, helping you start the inquiry process. The inquiry process can proceed similarly to this:

- What do I know?
- What does knowing tell me?
- What makes the most sense?
- What is possible?

Even with these public exercises, people would refuse to admit they didn't know when they didn't know. Those were the ones seeming to have confidence in themselves. What they had instead looked fearful, fear of not knowing, or fearful of admitting they didn't know. Fear always stifles the inquiry process. Fear provides a fixed frame of reference, not accommodating innovation and more expansive thinking. Expansive thinking is the birthing ground of ideas and innovation.

Once you can admit, *I don't know,* anything is possible. Isn't it?

I don't know is my most frequent starting point. When Audrey crumbled during her presentation, she asked me, "What do I do? I don't want this to happen again." I can answer the following:

- I don't know. What would you prefer to happen?
- If *that* happened, what would it do for you?
- What do you know about yourself to help you show up the way you want?

The inquiry process always leads to discovery: scientific discoveries, theological discoveries, philosophical discoveries, or personal discoveries. If *I don't know* is an ugly destination, try to think of it as a beautiful beginning.

It all begins with I don't know.

FAILURE
Don't try.
Try and fail.
Try and succeed.

Those are your options. When I was trying to lose weight, I kept failing. It got to the point where I stopped trying. If I stopped trying, I couldn't fail, and I also couldn't succeed. Fear of failure can be paralyzing. Failure scared me away. In certain professions, getting things wrong can be the difference between life and death. I think of my clinician clients and public servants. Failure or success, in a few fields, has a finality to it. Failure can alter another human being's existence.

Failure exists on a spectrum. There are many ways we can fail. I seem to have found an odd number of ways I can fail at losing weight. Looking at the failure to collect data got me excited about collecting data.

Pathways

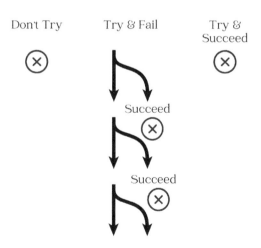

Figure 1. Your Success pathway includes three options: don't try, try and fail, and try and succeed. Trying and failing leads to more possibilities of trying and failing or trying and succeeding.

I tried a plant-based diet, intermittent exercise, not eating at night, weight clubs, professional trainers, meditation, prayer, and walking daily. I didn't start succeeding until I landed on what worked for me in the past, modified with new data I collected. When to eat was a lever I pulled in the past. Pulling the when-to-eat lever in the past worked for me, but not sustainably.

I found a healthy way to bring in nutrients and exercise. I played with the *when* component of eating with success. I wouldn't say I've figured out my weight loss regimen. Things may shift. In the past, when I failed, I thought, "it's not possible for me," or "my body doesn't work how anyone else's body works," or "past a certain age, weight loss is nearly impossible." While each of those statements may be true, none were helpful. None of those statements let me see my failure as a data point and information. Each of those statements was a judgment, not allowing me to see failure as an opportunity and a new starting point.

People think failure means you don't understand, are dumb, or perhaps your worst inner voice accuses you of many errors and all your past mistakes, which is the exact scenario Elaine faced.

ELAINE

Elaine hailed from a regulatory field. She was a senior vice president and the company expert in regulatory affairs. Various high-profile and urgent projects landed on her desk. Struggling to meet her deadlines, Elaine would tell herself she would get things wrong. Running through various possible scenarios of not getting things wrong meant she often missed deadlines. When she got something wrong, even a small error, she would ruminate over it, telling herself how awful she was at her job and that she couldn't get things right. Elaine found a personality she named a gatekeeper, keeping her stuck on the side of the fence where failure lived.

The gatekeeper reminded her to dig in her heels and check her work again to ensure everything was correct. Her peers were demanding a response to the urgent requests for the product application, and Elaine's gatekeeper wouldn't let her past the gate. After her gatekeeper encouraged her to put in ten to twelve-hour days, her gatekeeper wouldn't cheer or applaud her. If she managed to turn in perfect work, her gatekeeper wouldn't celebrate her. In these instances, the gatekeeper asked, "You took forever. Other people work much faster than you do!" In meetings, when she had a question, her gatekeeper would say, "Are you sure you want to ask such a dopey question? You might look a fool for asking such a simple question." It turned out that the chief marketing officer asked the same question ten minutes later. Elaine was in a no-win situation with her gatekeeper.

Elaine didn't know how to deal with her gatekeeper until she discovered she could look at failure similar to collecting data. She learned to pass through the gate as she told herself, "I'm collecting data." Elaine is learning to look at failure as data, not good data or bad data, simply data. Bye-bye Gatekeeper.

Elaine discovered a wider perspective where failure wasn't her character flaw. Failure became a data point. I invite you to see failure as collecting data.

ASSUME POSITIVE INTENT

Remember Ashley from marketing and media relations in the power chapter. Ashley had to deal with a demanding executive leader and felt powerless. She found her power had an air of crisp, clean linen smell. Her power was organizing. She knew the answers when she felt powerful, and power had a squeaky-clean sensation. She felt her powerful self emerge to address the executive leader. However, she lacked confidence. Power, poise, and presence tend to work in concert and not solo. While Ashley felt powerful and comfortable pushing back on the executive leader, she felt unsure of herself. She couldn't figure out why she doubted herself. When we discovered her presence, she found what she needed to banish her doubt.

What helped her discover how to erase her doubt was finding her confidence. Ashley learned to appreciate her presence biomarkers, "a sense of knowing I am right, I am organized, and my heart is leading me." When Ashley led with her heart, she discovered she wasn't at fault.

She told me, "He's a jerk. He really is. I feel sorry for him now. I see him differently. He's hurt and weak. Maybe his upbringing contributed to his having jerk tendencies. Maybe he didn't learn how to treat people." She found an appreciation and pity for her executive. She told me, "He is doing the best he can, and he doesn't have the greatest people skills."

When Ashley saw the jerk as doing the best he could, she viewed her situation with positive intent, meaning her first thought wasn't "something is wrong with me, or I am to blame." She found compassion for him and his situation. He was being a jerk and didn't know it. She became powerfully poised and present.

Once she could see him clearly, she discovered her role didn't align with her future. She had considered leaving because of him, and she told me, "I felt a failure because I couldn't figure out how to work with him. I see it really isn't him. Knowing what I've found changes everything."

"In what way?" I said.

"Now I know I need to leave, not because of him. All I saw before was him, and I wanted to run. I love the work and the people. Overall, a different field is calling me. What's changed is that I don't feel I'm running away. I have a purpose and a direction."

Her presence and strong confidence held deep wisdom, the power of understanding your power, poise, and presence. Your power, poise, and presence can communicate insightful findings, giving you counsel and advice. For them to serve you sage advice, you need to dust them off and let them shine.

POSSIBILITIES OF NOT KNOWING

In my thesis committee meeting, a professor asked me a question, and as I answered, I saw his face squiggling, telling me he didn't appreciate my answer. My confidence, similar to Audrey's, shattered. *I don't know the answer to anything*, I thought to myself. My internal communication was on overdrive. Red flags came up in my mind when I answered a question. I had doubts about the stuff I knew if I couldn't recall all the details from the citation. They didn't ask for the citation. They asked for my answer. I couldn't give it because I had this nagging doubt. Any emotion I had, I buried. Two hours later, I was unhappy with myself and disappointed in my performance.

If I would have said to myself when the professor had his squiggly face, "Wow, he has gas," or "Hmm, remember, not knowing is normal," or "If they give me the option to phone a friend, I am not phoning him," my experience changes. The outcome may or may not be different. Your experience will be different. It'll make all the difference in the world.

When you open yourself up to not knowing, the great unknown seems less scary. Being open to not knowing means you are open to possibilities and opportunities, an empowering position. You do not always need to know the correct answer. It would help if you were open to new ideas. You can't be open to new ideas if you have it all buttoned up.

Not knowing is normal.

Anything disturbing your confidence will impact your presence. Fear can disturb your confidence. Cassandra discovered how fear was holding her back.

PROVE IT. AGAIN?

"Hi, Cassandra. What did you bring for us today?" I said after Cassandra, and I had set up our first coaching meeting.

"I feel ready for my next role. I am kind of bored where I am now. I'm a high performer, and three years ago, my boss marked me for promotion to a director role. My organization had a reorg, and my boss went out the door. In came my new boss. I had to prove all over again that I had merited a promotion. At the end of the year, things looked good. He put me in for a promotion—another reorg. Out goes my boss out the revolving door, and in comes the new boss. Here I am, working toward a director role. Meanwhile, I'm doing the director's job," she said.

"Pardon?" I said.

"I'm a high performer. I've been taking on more responsibilities. I am *doing* the director role without a formal title or promotion. Another role came open in my organization for a director role. It was in a different area. I could do the job. I *like* my department. They hired someone for the role, and he has less experience than me!" she said, her hands waving in the air.

"I was talking to him the other day, and it turns out he doesn't have all the qualifications for the job like I do. He told me so. I am more qualified. I still don't have a director's role. They hired him from outside the company. Anyway, I'm in the situation now that I've got a new boss and I feel like I must prove myself all over again for a job I want. I want to know if I should stay in my current role and face another potential reorg or do something else," she said.

"Or something else. Cassandra, what's got you questioning?" I wondered.

She took a deep breath, and as she looked at her desk, she said, "Fear. It's fear." She took another deep breath and slowly recounted, "I didn't apply for the director role because it was in a different department. I want a director role, and I want it in my department. I love my department. I'm frustrated with my organization and the situation because I don't have the director role. Now I'm doing the director's role without the title, and the truth is, I've outgrown this role."

Cassandra's story is not an isolated one. Many Cassandras are out there facing a *prove it again* scenario. At the heart of a *prove it again* scenario is usually fear. Your career is in your hands. Make your decisions according to your chances of success.

You can call this situation *unfair* all day long. Cassandra chose not to apply for an open director's role. Many people feel like they are put in the position to demonstrate skills they've already shown before going after or being awarded promotions, a real obstacle for both men and women.

Student evaluations play a role in the career progression of professors. Students, however, rate women professors lower than male professors (Basow 2006; MacNell 2014). In several studies, both male and female raters rated female professors worse than male professors. Are women worse professors? It would appear not based on online research where they disguised the professor's gender identities (Boring 2016). The results of the disguised gender study with professors were similar to other studies where male and female student raters rated female professors lower than male professors. Are women held to a higher standard? Across the board, when students perceive the instructor is male, higher ratings follow. Are women professors held to a higher standard than their male peers, or is unconscious bias to blame (Hoorens 2020)?

WHY?

People often come to me and ask why. "Why didn't I get the job?" or "Why do I have to prove it again?" I don't know. I know this particular "why" can open wounds, hurts, and pains. These pains won't help my client get where they want to go. However, we shouldn't refrain from asking *why?*

When you do ask why I invite you to ask *why?* from a dispassionate place of curiosity. When you are in a dispassionate place of interest, you don't identify with the scenario, and you can study like a scientist without all the emotions draining you. Asking *why?* when your feelings or personal stakes are high will draw you in and bias your curious exploration.

For our curious work and the work you will need to do, we can overlook the *why?* as a bump in the road of your career. What do you do with bumps? I don't know about you. I drive around them, over them, adjust my driving tactics, sparing my car from taking a beating and my passengers, or I take a different route, one I may not like. I also alert the city they need to deal with this road hazard.

Whatever the cause, you will need resilience to navigate these "bumps" along your personal and professional life.

FACING FEAR

Until the city fixes the road, we have work to do creating your plan to deal with your bumps.

Cassandra shared with me, "When I look at it from the perspective of a hiring manager, he (the director) brings knowledge of our competitor. I don't have his knowledge, critical for the role he took. I didn't apply for the role. I can't complain I have to prove it again. I *told* myself I had to prove it—every time. Instead of applying for roles inside and outside of my company, I let fear stop me from trying to get where I want to go. I didn't even try, Lizette."

Be powerfully present and brave. Face your fear.

FOMO

In chapter 1, I shared a question arising after a workshop I gave. A brave participant asked, "How can I avoid the fear of missing out pushing me to attend all these meetings?"

Is your calendar filled with meetings? Can you sympathize with the statement from my workshop participant?

FOMO stands for fear of missing out. Fear is a compelling motivator. I asked the brave participant what they were experiencing, and she said, "I have a team, and my responsibilities touch many areas, and often others do not invite me to meetings where I need information. I learn about these meetings and attend to catch the one or two possible items that connect with my work. If I don't attend, what happens is I find out about those things too late, and I must rush to correct or put in place the needed work."

Let me see if I understand. "You attend meetings no one invited you to attend. There is essential information provided at these meetings touching your responsible areas. If you don't attend, you won't find out until a later time when the need is critical. When the need is critical, you rush to fix what no one informed you about."

"Yes."

"What happens if you don't rush to fix what no one told you was needed from you?" I said. Pausing for a moment seeing a perplexed look, I continued, "Two things come to mind. When you rush around fixing what no one informed you, the people responsible for not telling you face no consequences. They feel no pain. You are feeling the pain, rushing to fix what you didn't know because no one told you. Now you are attending meetings, halfway listening while you do other work in the hopes of catching what their needs are from you, losing critical time you could be using to do your focused work."

She nodded.

I continued, "This information doesn't sound critical to your management responsibilities. Your other option is to send a delegate in your place."

"You're right; I don't need to be the one attending all these meetings, and I hadn't thought of letting things fail to fix my situation. Once others feel the pain, they might inform me next time," she said.

My brave, inquisitive participant didn't have a fear of missing out. She didn't want to fail. I used a poise power tool of pausing to reflect and a presence power tool of exploring failure. Failure can be good (Grant 2021). Failure is what leaders must encourage others not to fear. Leaders question, challenge, and encourage different thinking leading to innovation. Good leaders encourage by being thought partners to others, not judging or ridiculing, but rather helping others see what they might be missing.

There are times not to embrace failure to teach others lessons. A dangerous situation is not a time to explore failure; an uncomfortable one is. When you have power, poise, and presence, you communicate with clarity, embrace ambiguity or discomfort with an ability to pause, and embrace failure or success, knowing neither is your identity. Be willing to fail. Be willing to allow others to fail.

MAUREEN

When Maureen from chapter 4 noted, "it's easy for me to say that here, how do I say it at work?" what would you tell her?

Maureen didn't know about her power, poise, or presence. If she had, I might have said, "Your power, poise, and presence space is yours. No one else can take it from you unless you choose to let them." Even if you need to share tough feedback, when you lead from your zone of power, poise, and presence, you'll share the feedback with authenticity. When you need to speak uncomfortable truths, remember to:

- Reframe your situation. Who else is more uncomfortable or more afraid to speak up than you? Who needs you to be brave and model how to speak in discomfort?
- Expand your vision. Who else will benefit from your speaking?
- Embrace your discomfort. It's normal to be uncomfortable. It's a sign of growth.
- Collect data. Failure is good at giving you data.
- Tell yourself that not knowing is normal. You don't know how others will respond. There is often more than one possible outcome. What if the best outcome was to happen?

In the next chapters, we'll explore leading from your power, poise, and presence zone. We will do power, poise, and presence polishing in the next chapters.

AUTHENTIC LEADERSHIP

CHAPTER TWELVE

Authentic Leadership

In the middle of every difficulty lies opportunity.

—ALBERT EINSTEIN

"I have no more f***s to give," said Tanya.

"Pardon my language, but at this stage in my career, I will no longer be someone else, trying to make others happy, doing things that don't matter to me, and leaving myself for last," said Tanya.

Authentic leadership is being genuine and sincere about who you are as an individual. Being authentic involves matching your private persona with your public persona and reducing your energy consumption because you aren't switching personas from one area of your life to another. With a fast pace of change and increasing public visibility of your activities, maintaining a genuine persona is someone positioned to inspire trust and loyalty.

Authentic leadership is at the intersection of power, poise, and presence. Cultivating your power, poise, and presence means practicing using your biomarkers and finding power, poise, and presence moments and opportunities. Recognizing moments allows you the chance to flex your biomarker muscles. Once you've identified your biomarkers, you can explore working with them as a unit, taking you to new places.

AUTHENTIC LEADERSHIP BIOMARKERS

Your biomarkers are unique to you. No one else has your life experiences, not even your twin if you are a twin. Your experiences can be good fuel for your power, poise, and presence biomarkers. Anywhere in your power, poise, and presence space is your authentic leadership. Hereafter I'll suggest that the overlap of power, poise, and presence is your authentic leadership zone or your zone.

I've had multiple clients identify biomarkers for their characteristics the same as for their opposite characteristics. The difference was that one was stagnant and the other flowing. I've also had multiple clients identify unique biomarkers for characteristics and their opposites. Biomarkers aren't right or wrong. Your biomarkers reflect your uniqueness and your wealth of past experiences. Once you identify your biomarkers, they are yours to explore, name, and put to work for you.

RECOGNIZE

The first step in practicing using your authentic leadership is to bring your power, poise, and presence biomarkers together and begin to work with them outside of crucial moments when you need to be in your zone. Eventually, you'll be able to bring your authentic leadership into your critical moments, similar to executing a play on game day.

Players don't coordinate game moves on game day. Players practice and perfect their game moves on the training field. Your authentic leadership zone biomarkers are no different. Your biomarkers are unique to you, and as such, they resonate with you in a way no one else will recognize. No one else will experience what you experience when your authentic leadership biomarkers are present or not present.

To bring all your authentic leadership zone biomarkers together, bring each one to your mind with your power, poise, and presence assessments or recipe cards. Don't worry if you have similarities between characteristics. They overlap, and since they overlap, you might experience the same biomarker for multiple traits. Remind yourself what each characteristic includes. Reflect on:

- Your posture
- Feelings from your characteristics
- Where your characteristics center
- Any motion associated with each characteristic
- Any additional sensations

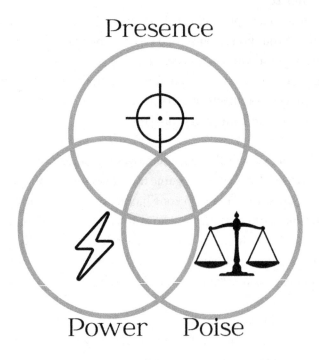

Figure 1. Power, poise, and presence overlap. The area where all three overlap is your authentic leadership zone.

The next step is to consider power, poise, and presence together and determine your consolidated zone biomarkers at the intersection of power, poise, and presence. This is the sweet spot where your authentic leadership zone lives. In this space of all three of your characteristics, you can complete your inventory assessment to determine your high-level biomarkers, such as

- Posture. What is your posture when all three characteristics, power, poise, and presence, are present?

- What is different with this feeling, if anything?
- What attributes does your zone have?
- What is your authentic leadership center?
- What if any motion exists?
- What additional sensations arise for you?

When you have finished reflecting on your recipe cards and recalling your power, poise, and presence, notice what sensations arise. Notice your posture, sensations, and especially the source of your authentic leadership. By reflecting on these sensations, you will have assembled your zone biomarkers.

When you're in your authentic leadership zone, your best power, poise, and presence biomarkers are alive. Repeat the above exercise if you struggle at all until you settle on your authentic leadership's best and move forward. You can always revisit and refine. Fill out your authentic leadership zone recipe card with your discoveries.

My authentic leadership zone occurs when I am upright and loose. There is a lightness surrounding me. I feel my power, poise, and presence centered below my heart as if a drop of water hits a pond and sends waves outward. Another sensation I have become aware of is openness. My skin tingles, and I have a higher sense of awareness.

LIZETTE'S AUTHENTIC
LEADERSHIP ZONE

Posture _Upright and loose_
Feels Like _lightness_
Center _Below heart_
Motion _Ripples around me, agility_
Sensation _awareness, openness, skin tingles_

Figure 2. Lizette's authentic leadership recipe card.

You can use the authentic leadership recipe card to note your biomarker for your recall later. This will form the basis for developing and strengthening your ability to bring these characteristics to life at any moment.

194 · POWER, POISE, AND PRESENCE

Posture_____
Feels Like_____
Center_____
Motion_____
Sensation_____

Figure 3. Your authentic leadership recipe card.

NOW WHAT?

You have discovered your power, poise, presence, and your authentic leadership. What remains? Quite a lot. This is the beginning.

Discovering your zone biomarkers is a starting point. The real work is where you put the learning into action, changing your life, and stepping into your powerful, poised, and present self in all your moments of each day. A few recommendations for starting your tangible work follow.

SLOW DOWN

When working at breakneck speed, you don't notice bodily sensations. Research shows that most people hold their breath or have shallow breaths when doing a simple work activity, such as responding to an email (Leone 201; Stone 2014). Chances are you are blissful and unaware of this vital process for life when you're focusing intently on work. This breath-hold scenario builds up stress factors due to your body's balance of oxygen, carbon dioxide, and nitric oxide, mediating your body's response to inflammation, affecting your ability to fight infection, and hindering your robust immune system (Stone 2014).

If you can't maintain awareness of your breath, how will you track how you are feeling at any moment? Practice. Deliberate practice when you are not in a crucial moment will help you face a real-world challenge to staying in your zone.

MAKING YOUR BIOMARKERS WORK FOR YOU

After having explored your authentic leadership biomarkers, you might have a feel for them. Exercising your authentic leadership biomarkers will help you stay in the zone. Exploring your authentic leadership from the point of view of your biomarkers is what's next. Strengthening your ability to lean into your zone when specific biomarkers are already present will make it easier for you to get into your authentic leadership. We want to do the work to bring your authentic leadership to life when none of the biomarkers are present. Identifying your authentic leadership recipe card gives us a place to start.

Let's assume you have identified your authentic leadership and discovered your presence and confident space. Your presence has biomarkers. We'll use the following for simplicity:

Posture: Standing up

It feels as if: I'm in charge, positive

Attributes: Prepared, focused thoughts

Center: Head and heart

Motion: Equal movement between head and heart

Sensation: We are in conversation, listen to the other, and are both curious

Let's also assume you are going to a meeting and are nervous because you aren't sure you'll have anything enlightening to say. In the past, perhaps you've been quick to lose confidence when you sense someone isn't listening to you. Your presence has the above biomarkers. When you feel thrown off course and start to unravel, sensing someone isn't listening to you, your presence can vanish. In the past, you might have felt derailed because, right or wrong, you sensed the conversation wasn't going the way you wanted it to go. Your confidence slips, and you begin to lose your presence.

What if when you sense you've lost your audience and they are no longer interested, you instead assume the conversation is on the right course, regardless of the feedback you believe you are getting? You would take your biomarkers, positive, prepared, focused thoughts, and stay with those regardless of what you believe you see or experience. Perhaps you misread the signs of your audience, or you misinterpreted those signs.

Regardless, you affirm to yourself,

- positive
- prepared
- focused thoughts
- I am in charge
- we are in conversation
- we listen
- we are both curious

Maybe the person has an upset stomach. Maybe the other person fought with their spouse or is in the middle of a divorce. Maybe your audience has a few other things on their mind. If you carry on assuming your audience is curious and further assume they are listening to you, you might keep hold of your confidence and stay present. If you maintain a grasp on your confidence when your audience decides to tune back in, they will find you are still engaged and engaging. You may have led them with your maintained composure. Chances are you can turn the corner and continue to have great dialogue. In either case, you continue in presence, regardless of the circumstances.

DRINKING FROM THE WELLSPRING

If you lose your authentic leadership at any moment, chances are you could spiral out of control. In truth, you can lose any characteristic. We are choosing to pick on your authentic leadership.

Substitute your own Achilles heel characteristic if you prefer. It's a steeper road to climb back without some biomarkers present. You can make your authentic leadership zone appear from nothing, and we'll address this in the following exercise. For the moment, try to catch the slipping authentic leadership zone in the moment by bringing to mind your biomarkers and drinking from the wellspring.

You will avoid spiraling out of control, and you'll look positive and in charge (or your biomarkers).

NOTICE

The first step to practicing your zone is to notice in your workday how often those zone biomarkers, in whole or in part, are natural and present. We will now revisit the biomarker tracker introduced earlier because you can deploy this tracker with your zone in mind.

Authentic Leadership Biomarker Tracker

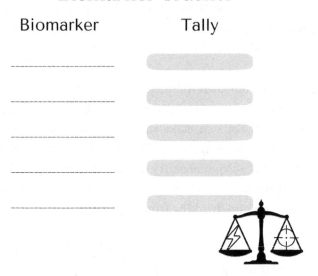

Figure 4. Your authentic leadership biomarker tracker.

After logging and tracking your biomarkers, reflect on the moments sticking out for you when your biomarkers were present. Occasionally, a client will feel a particular biomarker relates to a physical location, memory, or time of day. You may encounter a theme. Practice noticing where, when, or under what conditions particular zone biomarkers are strong for you. These are the wellsprings you can revisit to fill up your biomarkers.

I have a coffee cup, my absolute favorite. I picked it up from Finland during a business trip. The distinctive two-tone bold color and the floral pattern remind me of Finland, the hiking, the people, nature, and my friends and colleagues.

I worked in a high-performing organization based in Finland, and we transformed multiple times. It was the first time in my life that I was ever part of a high-performing team. Many times, I considered myself part of high-performing teams. Often, people think this. You don't know you are in a high-performing team until you are no longer part of the team. Until you unlock high performance and are in the flow, not as an individual but as an organization, and reflect in hindsight, can you tell if a team is a high-performing one or not. We award medals at the end of a race, not in the middle of one.

The department no longer exists. I embody the openness, high-performance characteristics, and interdependence of our team when I look at or hold my Finnish cup. My cup is one of my wellsprings. Knowing what, where or when your biomarkers or authentic leadership moments occur can serve as your wellspring refill location.

Use a zone biomarker tracker to notice in hindsight those moments where your authentic leadership biomarkers are present. Learn to discover when or where your biomarkers occur and what makes your biomarkers emerge. In this way, you can learn to cultivate your wellsprings.

Zone Moment Tracker

Biomarker	Moment or Location
_____	☐
_____	☐
_____	☐
_____	☐

Figure 5. Authentic leadership moment tracker to track authentic leadership biomarkers and moments.

RECALL YOUR BIOMARKER

Another way to cultivate your authentic leadership besides the previous exercise is to bring it to mind. This is one way to make your authentic leadership zone appear out of thin air. Your memory serves an important purpose. Your memory isn't a simple repository of information. Your catalog of living, envisioned, or imagined experiences reside in your memory banks.

You can do the following exercise with any moment or experience where you showed up as fully you, or you can recatalog an experience. Recall your biomarkers or an experience of your authentic leadership or even a future one where you show up exactly as you would imagine. Read your recipe card, pausing to say each biomarker aloud. Recall the experience of the characteristic. The deeper and richer your experience, the better you can capture and relive it.

When bringing your biomarkers to mind, be curious. Under what conditions was your experience? Who was nearby? What were you doing? How were you feeling? What were you sensing? What was happening? Make the memory as vivid as possible with the intention of latching onto your authentic leadership.

Figure 6. Authentic leadership memory. Use the space to capture a past authentic leadership memory or create a future one.

HANG ON

Hang on or latch on to your authentic leadership zone. Once you find your zone, tag it and step into it because it's yours. For me, I drink deep from my coffee cup when I need a dose of high performance. I'm an experienced and trained coach. I allow doubt to creep into my life and coaching mind, not something I'm proud to admit.

However, when those moments strike, I will, by instinct, reach for my coffee cup, whether it's full or empty, and drink in my high-performance zone. When my coffee cup is empty, I can drink deeply, all the way down to my toes, as I prepare to coach my full attention-seeking CEO. When I put down the coffee cup, my high-performing self is present again.

My authentic leadership latch is a coffee cup. For Bette Midler, it was sharp-heeled shoes. For you, it can be a scarf, necklace, glasses, opening your laptop, putting your hand on your heart, a word, a prayer, or something else. Your *latch* is specific to you. Make your zone latch tangible and use your visual, auditory, and sensory perceptions to create a new experience you can draw from whenever you need it.

REJOICE

The first moments of creating a habit are crucial (Fogg 2019). Rejoice the first few times you latch onto your authentic leadership zone. Your zone latch deserves a celebration because this celebratory behavior will ensure your latching is successful. You'll be able to dig it up easier the next time you need your authentic leadership.

It takes my husband, on average, a quarter of an hour to get me out of the house for any event. I use those precious moments to locate my wallet, keys, socks, shoes, and purse, and sometimes I continue working until he walks out the door. I will swear up and down that someone moved whatever it is I lost. The truth is those things don't matter to me. I leave them anywhere and everywhere. As a result, I'm not quite sure where they are when I need them. I locate my favorite scarf easily because it's always on my desk when it's not on my neck.

My favorite coffee cup is on my desk unless I'm washing it. I don't lose either of them, ever. All else, I tend to lose. I kept losing my headphones, I found them a home, and I put them in their home, saying, "Wow, what a nice feeling knowing where they are!" I don't know if I really feel nice because I don't care for headphones. When I say it feels nice, the weight comes off my shoulders. This is how I rejoice when I'm starting a habit. Rejoice in your new-formed and growing zone habit.

MAKING YOUR BIOMARKERS APPEAR. MAGIC.

When some of your biomarkers are present, showing up with authentic leadership is easier. When your authentic leadership biomarkers aren't present, showing up in the zone is challenging.

Let's assume you've had a tough day with many setbacks, and with a sudden prompting, you must present the latest new venture to stakeholders. The venture news does not look good. You are not feeling your power, poise, or presence, or authentic leadership. You want to run and hide. What do you do in this situation?

We will make your authentic leadership magically appear. You have already been practicing making your authentic leadership zone appear if you've been doing the thought experiments in this chapter, especially the previous exercise. In fact, you've been practicing with your authentic leadership muscle as you've made your way through this book. The stretch is to make your authentic leadership zone appear in a stressful moment when you need your authentic best the most. We have worked with individual biomarkers making up your authentic leadership and in non-stressful moments.

When stress strikes, reflect on your authentic leadership biomarkers, moments, or memories. Sam from chapter 6 would tense and tighten her shoulders when she felt powerless, knowing she was showing up without poise or presence. Her voice would go hoarse, and she'd start coughing. We worked on a single biomarker, relaxing her shoulders in times of stress. One of her authentic leadership biomarkers was that she relaxed her shoulders, and she discovered that when stress consumed her, she'd tighten up her shoulders to her ears.

Sam practiced keeping her shoulders down during stress and discovered that her authentic leadership zone became easier for her. The stress didn't leave or disappear. Her ability to manage stress scaled upward when she got her body in the right frame of reference. Sam found her shoulders relaxed, and it banished her coughing spells and hoarse voice. Sam noticed she still felt anxious and nervous.

Her anxiety had scaled back by keeping her shoulders down. Relaxing her shoulders was an intentional decision on her part and the one thing she brought to mind when she found herself in the middle of a stressful encounter. This became her small step, leading to huge successes for her. As a leader, she couldn't remove the stressful encounters in her day. She could change the way she reacted.

Sam changed how her body responded. This, in turn, decreased her perceived stress level. She changed her stress level downward for those around her, in her organization, and for herself. You can do a similar activity.

WORKING YOUR MAGIC

Find an authentic leadership biomarker you can commit to strengthening in moments of stress or difficulty for the next two weeks. Perhaps the biomarker you choose is a sense of connectedness. In a meeting or encounter you find challenging, stay focused on connecting to the speaker, connect your fingers together, and feel the friction between your fingers, or rest a hand on your belly to connect to your breath. These are some ideas of how you can use your biomarkers to make authentic leadership appear for you. I chose connectedness. You choose the biomarkers and ways to make the biomarker appear for you.

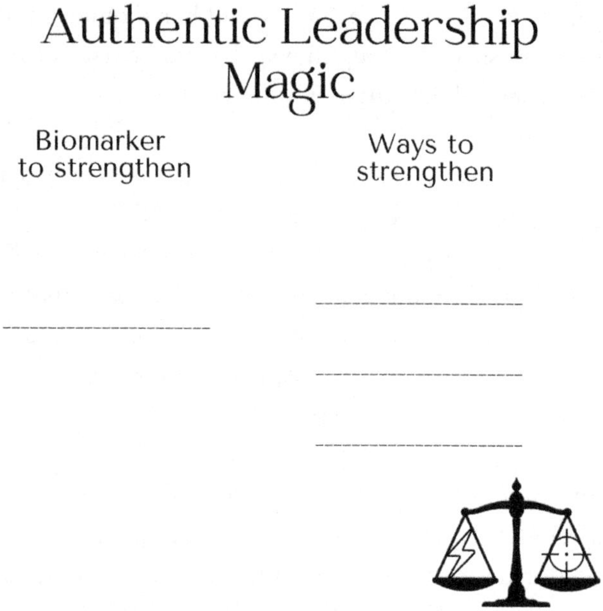

Authentic Leadership Magic

Biomarker
to strengthen

Ways to
strengthen

Figure 7. Authentic Leadership Magic practice. Identify an authentic leadership biomarker and ways to strengthen this biomarker to practice making your authentic leadership appear.

REFINING YOUR AUTHENTIC LEADERSHIP
BIOMARKERS

On occasion, you can revisit and refine your authentic leadership biomarkers. You are a being of your experiences, and as you grow and stretch, you catalog more experiences. Biomarker discoveries today may be less relevant to you a year from now when you've been practicing your authentic leadership. You can use the above exercises to prune or shape your authentic leadership biomarkers as you grow and stretch.

REFINE

Wendy from chapter 7 discovered self-care, mama bear. She identified the smell of freshly baked cookies as part of her poise. We discovered later that the cookies belonged. The cookie smell didn't. If a biomarker is wishful thinking, the biomarker won't feel right when you voice it aloud or practice with it.

Your authentic leadership biomarkers aren't static. They may take on a smell, taste, or experience different from what you've outlined during your journey through *Power, Poise, and Presence.* Your characteristics may also shed an attribute or two along the way. I encourage you to revisit your biomarkers. Aside from shifting or changing, your biomarkers may reveal deeper insights, or they may reveal when you are ready for your next promotion or career leap. Your authentic leadership biomarkers can indicate when a role is a good or bad fit for you or what new direction to take and when to take it.

Next, we take on imbalances in your power, poise, and presence.

CHAPTER THIRTEEN

Energy Efficiency

———

When you ask and show others how to help, you are modeling
leadership. Leadership gives first and receives second.
—DR. LIZETTE WARNER (CHAPTER 10)

"Being in charge doesn't mean I know what to do. Everyone assumes I have the answers and am making decisions
all day. I'm exhausted. I have this pit in my stomach. Am I
doing what I am supposed to? Are we going to make it past
this quarter and next? How will we meet our orders? I'm
sleeping poorly, and everyone is tugging at me," said Will at
the start of our conversation. It was somewhat similar to my
discussion with Emma.

"You have to help me on how to manage. I'm left on my own.
No one is giving me directions, instructions, or even assistance. I get more to do and have to devise plans without
guidance. I'm doing the work, missing key conversations I
don't know how to have. I didn't even have a performance
review or development discussion with anyone for myself. Is

this normal? How am I supposed to lead when I don't even feel I belong?"

The situations Will and Emma were experiencing have a commonality: gaps. Will had a poise gap, while Emma had a power gap. How can you make power, poise, and presence work for you in a similar situation Will or Emma were experiencing? I've found that capturing these three, power, poise, and presence, isolates your authentic leadership zone. Throughout our exploration, you may have found that some of the biomarkers for power, poise, or presence seem similar or are in common. The biomarkers overlap, as you have discovered. How they overlap for you can shed additional light on how to lean into your authentic leadership zone.

Often my clients will note their power has similar, however, not the same features to their poise, for example. The overlap is essential for your power, poise, and presence. Grasping these overlaps and gaps will help you fine-tune and serve as a clue for your authentic leadership energy efficiency, allowing you to manage your authentic leadership.

An imbalance in your authentic leadership can occur when a single characteristic overpowers the other two. I refer to this instance as *leading with* a particular characteristic. We'll cover leading with first, followed by when a single characteristic is emerging into two steady or stronger ones.

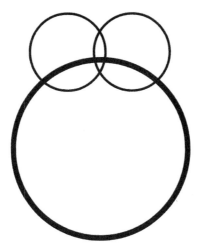

Figure 1. Graphical representation of leading with one characteristic, demonstrating the authentic leadership footprint, the space inside the circles is small.

LEADING WITH

One characteristic (power, poise, or presence) standing on its own, stronger than the other two, indicates a weakness of the other two characteristics. In this case, you may be muscling through your zone, working harder than you need to work. You may have even gotten accustomed to this circumstance. In this case, your zone can be power-heavy, poise-heavy, or presence-heavy, reducing your authentic leadership footprint.

LEADING WITH POWER

"Drop and give me twenty," I heard the commander tell his trainees.

Leading with power can show up like barking orders. Someone leading with power may seem comfortable in the space of power. They may fake presence or poise. These people may have convinced themselves that they are the essence of authentic leadership when in power or wielding power, and when losing power, they can blame or shame others.

Ravi, CEO of his company, led with power. When he had a workforce reduction and had to let people go, he blamed the workers for it. He called them lazy and the source of the company's weakness. Ravi couldn't and wouldn't see anything from anyone else's perspective. Ravi had to take a leave of absence because of his actions.

When my father stormed into a burning house to get the girls stuck in the house out, he led with power. It was an emergency. Lives were in danger. There are times when you will need to lead with power. However, if leading with power is your default mode, you may want to examine if adding presence or poise might make your life easier by expanding your authentic leadership zone.

LEADING WITH POISE

When I was a young girl and the only one left home with mom and dad, I learned how to lead with poise. Mom and dad were constantly bickering, nothing dangerous or violent, undoubtedly voluminous. I was the one trying to keep the peace and resolve disagreements. I hated arguments and discord and was the one brokering peace.

Leading with poise can seem a good thing. Someone leading with poise can be comfortable in the space of balance and getting to balance. They might release any powerful traits for the greater peace-making or balance cause. They may lose confidence in their ideas or strategies or refrain from asking hard questions to stay in their poise space. This person may allow another's ideas forward, even if they disagree, to keep the status quo. When you lead with poise, it might lead to you believing everyone else is correct, and you have no voice.

When I led with poise alone, I felt alone. Sure I brokered peace, not true peace. To broker true peace, you are willing to ask powerful questions, be uncomfortable, allow things to fall apart, and have the confidence to know the issue will resolve, however, not in the way you expect.

LEADING WITH PRESENCE

"Shut up and sit down," commanded the irritated comedian. Security guards ran to escort the boisterous attendee out of the venue.

Leading with presence shows up similar to the comedian I witnessed, leaving the audience shaken by how he handled a rowdy patron. To lead with presence means you might be confident in yourself or comfortable in the space where you have or appear to have confidence. Your aura can be palpable, full of self-assuredness. Being strong in presence and low on power or power tools, this person may lack the ability to hang onto their power during uncertainty.

Since the overlap with poise is weak, they may feel off-balanced stepping out of their confident presence space. They may fake confidence or grip it tightly. The fear of losing presence can be upsetting or stressful. They may not have room for others' ideas or suggestions because they lack the poise to remain balanced in the space where they might be wrong.

If you've seen Frank Caliendo, a sports and impression comedian, you know he works impressions from his audience into his live performances (Caliendo 2018). He seems to thrive on enlisting the audience in his act. He pivots into a different impression direction at a cue from his audience. He manages from the stage with incredible presence, not letting his presence dominate his act because his poise in pivoting and his powerful communication make his actions seem effortless. This effortlessness happens when power, poise, and presence are in equal balance.

WHAT TO DO IF YOU LEAD WITH

Suppose you become aware you are leading with anything. Congratulations! You've taken a huge step. Once you become aware of leading with a characteristic, you can begin to notice all the different ways it is serving and not serving you. Continue to notice. After noticing, do nothing. It's a suggestion, one rooted in deep experience. Rushing to do and fix may contribute to making the situation worse.

The next step after noticing would be to play with imagining living a life with one or the other characteristics you are missing. You may notice a gap filling with a different characteristic.

You can try a new behavior in line with your weaker characteristics. To do this, you can use your recipe cards. Experimenting will lead to results allowing you to fine-tune your new behavior. For trying something new, whether it works or not, rejoice.

Rejoice whether you are successful or not. Any small token of appreciation for your attempt is sufficient (a smile, a clap, a thumbs up, a dance). Having experimented with something new, you will have data informing you what your next step should be.

As an example, I did this:

- I notice I favor leading with poise.
- I start to notice when I lead with poise, leading me to see that "keeping the peace" becomes my priority. For example, I handled an urgent situation because I had the skill to do it even though the task wasn't in my domain. This led to the responsible person not knowing about the urgent situation or feeling pressured to address the urgency. Next time the same thing happens. In keeping the peace, I missed an opportunity to share essential knowledge or skills with others by not engaging the expert owning the situation.
- What are my options:
  - Continue.
  - Lean into my presence to let the work land on the responsible person's desk. They will feel the pressure.
  - I may need to ask a powerful question or get more comprehensive visibility on this problem.
  - Ask for help. This is a presence move.

- I try a different option than my go-to behavior.
  - I gathered data on how an option worked out for me.
    - I can decide to keep a behavior or try a different option.
- Rejoice! I did something new.
- Fine-tune it.

Here is a short process flow:

- Notice.
- Do nothing. Notice what happens.
- Discover your options.
- Play with options.
- Try a new behavior.
- Fine-tune a new behavior.
- Celebrate your attempt and return to earlier steps, depending on your situation.
- Continue to fine-tune.

You may find the new behavior feels light and takes up less energy, a bonus of strengthening your weaker characteristics.

WHAT TO DO IF YOU NOTICE SOMEONE ELSE IS LEADING WITH?

This is frequently the question posed by others noticing right away that someone else is leading with a characteristic. My response is, "What would you wish for yourself?" If someone sees you lead with power, for example, what will cause you to appreciate yourself and the person giving you this information? This is an excellent place to put down the book, pause, and reflect to find your answer.

If you took the opportunity to pause and reflect, you might have several options popping up for you. I would suggest working with one of those options. However, I would be remiss if I didn't provide at least a few options for you if you find yourself in this situation. The following are several suggestions:

- **Drop any pretense you need to fix anything**
  This is a tough one worth mentioning. We can rarely change people by pointing it out, suggesting they do something different, or telling them they have a problem. Chances are, if they have a problem, they are well aware of their problem or stuck with a resolution.

  If your life is miserable due to their actions or inactions, you don't have to like your situation. You can address what *you* will do about your case. Your situation is different from theirs. How you respond is up to you.

- **Appreciate them**
  Having compassion for someone else is one of the most beautiful gifts we can give ourselves and others. You, too, were once in a position of being a bucket head. It doesn't matter if they are fifty years old and should know better.

- **Model the behavior**
  People are always watching you. Even when you think they aren't watching. Humans have a tremendous capacity to learn and adapt. When you model behaviors, others watch and learn. If you aren't demanding someone else change, they might even begin to play with some of the

things you do well. *Praise any attempt they try.* Don't wait for perfection. Encourage growth with praise.

You may become the one others admire.

- **Invite change**
  You only receive an invitation after a relationship is present. I don't think someone has ever invited me to a birthday party when I didn't know a soul. I may have only known the organizer. I knew someone. If you don't have a relationship, you can't provide an invitation effectively. If you model the behavior, have patience, and build a relationship of trust, they may ask you for advice or your opinion, your moment to invite change. Tell them what they are doing well. Inquire about what they think is missing.

- **Listen**
  Listen to their response and provide one invitation to change. This invitation could be something similar to, "I agree with you. It seems you are losing your audience by sticking firmly to your point. May I offer a suggestion, or do you already know what to do?" If they haven't had a brainstorm and are accepting your offer, then provide one.

- **Challenge**
  Lean into your authentic leadership and supply a challenge. Shops, advertisers, and businesses often offer challenges: a three-day sale, a thirty-day workout challenge, etc. You could do the same.

IMBALANCE

An imbalance appears when two characteristics are present, and the third is weak or nonexistent. There are different types of inequalities. Power and poise may be strong while presence is weak, or power and presence are dominant while poise is lagging, or poise and presence are powerful while power isn't.

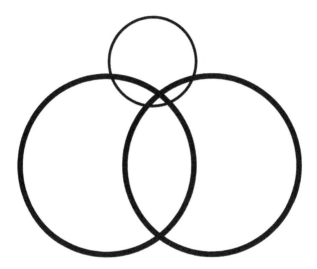

Figure 2. A graphical representation when two characteristics dominate a weaker characteristic, demonstrating space to grow your authentic leadership footprint, the area within the circles.

How can you address an imbalance if you notice you have one?

EMERGING CHARACTERISTICS

The case of a single weak overlap or a lagging characteristic deserves attention because, in my experience, this is a stage of growth many of us will pass through. You should celebrate if you get to a dual overlap because you are close to maturing your authentic leadership. I say mature because maturation comes in stages. When you think maturation is complete, a new phase begins. With the tools you've learned throughout this book, you'll be able to direct the growth and balance of your authentic leadership, even when changing over time.

THE POWER-POISE OVERLAP

Someone with power and poise overlapping may be the most influential person in their part of the organization or department. They may have to balance various stakeholders, competing demands, trends, and competition. Balancing all those things is a magic act. They might make their work seem effortless. What they may lack is presence. Leaders growing and maturing to new levels shed old skills to bring new skills on board. For example, a team leader may have been a subject matter expert. The leader will have to shed her subject matter expertise to learn how to lead her team. She cannot do the team's work if she is the team leader. She must orchestrate the group's work, a different skill from being an individual contributor.

In some cases, leaders must relearn skills. For example, they may need to relearn subject matter expertise skills for high-performing teams. You may no longer be the subject matter expert in a new role. You may lack the confidence to act because you are no longer the subject matter expert you've relied upon. Confidence can ebb and flow or might easily disappear. Someone with a solid power-poise overlap may doubt themselves and feel their confidence is weak.

My clients with strong power and poise have commented, "Presence seems the shakiest of all three." What are you to do if this applies to you?

THE PRESENCE PULL-UP

If power and poise are strong for you, you may be able to lean into power, and poise, to loop in your presence. How might you do this? Pulling in a third is easier if you hang onto your two-thirds majority. You don't need all your presence. With some practice in a safe space, you can make incremental progress to boost your presence by doing a presence pull-up.

Here are a few suggestions:

1. Build up your power and poise by using your recipe cards. Once power and poise are engaged, notice what presence is in this space for you.

2. Practice with your presence biomarkers or recipe card when in the presence of power and poise. Doing this is similar to riding a bike. The more you practice, the more you intuitively course-correct when you are getting wobbly, and the easier it becomes. The easiest way to practice would be to take a few minutes a day when brushing your teeth and bring to mind your power and your poise. Review your presence recipe card. Notice the

new feelings and give yourself a celebratory pat on the back to strengthen your confidence in yourself.

3. It may seem counterintuitive to lean into your poise, your strength of not knowing. Leaning into your poise can help you by affirming that your situation will turn out well, although you may not know how. Remember, perfect poise is not perfect. Perfect poise recognizes you may not know. Your presence may be the very thing you need to navigate yourself or your team through unknowns. You may not have all the answers. Your poise can help you be confident, knowing you have the right people or can find them.

THE POWER-PRESENCE OVERLAP

I don't know if there was a single CEO comfortable with the unknowns the pandemic threw at their companies. Someone with a solid power-presence overlap may be most uncomfortable navigating the discomfort of unknowns with poise. How do you stay singing to a tune when the music has stopped, and the expectation is for you to continue singing? This happened to me in the choir.

During one of our practices, our choir director instructed the organist, Mr. Todd, to stop while she was expecting the choir to continue. I remember feeling uncomfortable. My naked voice was out there for all to hear. My poise and the poise of my fellow choir members were tested. Poise can be the most fragile of the power, poise, and presence triad, requiring calm and balance when the unknown has happened and you're naked or feel naked.

During a virtual group workshop, my screen share decided it would not cooperate with me. I pushed the button. Nothing happened. I kept singing, except, in this case, I was speaking and presenting with the attitude that the slides hadn't had a hiccup. I ignored the technical glitch and continued the story. I engaged my poise while telling the story of poise and sharing poise tools. Had I orchestrated this, I couldn't have planned it any better. While my screen share wouldn't work, we continued our conversation in the group. Technology sometimes doesn't play nice, and you are powerless to do anything about it. In the middle of one of my last sentences, the screen share decided to work. Smoothly, I slipped my conversation into matching the slides.

Our group noticed this unplanned modeling of poise, and we ended up having a breakout on this topic. Had I planned on it, I am confident I would have been disingenuous. This poise moment was all the more powerful because it was unplanned. Sometimes it takes seeing a model in action to know what you wish to develop in yourself.

Having a target doesn't make working with poise easy. However, having a target does give you a goal. Experimenting with poise in conjunction with power and presence will help you develop your skill to wrangle your poise into action.

THE POISE SONG

Similar to the presence pull-up, you'll find singing with poise easier when you have two-thirds of the choir. Here are a few ways I've used to strengthen poise.

1. Known unknowns. Your car will run out of fuel. The vehicle running out of fuel is a known unknown because *when* the fuel runs out depends on various things.

   There are also unknown unknowns. I did not think we would welcome an Irish Wolfhound into our home. Unknown unknowns are unknown. Since unknowns will occur, they are certain, making them known even if you don't know what they are. This means you can plan for the unknown. What is it? I don't know. When will it happen? Also, I don't know. How will it happen? I don't know. Will it happen? Yes. I can plan for the unknown, even if I don't know when it will happen or what it will be. I know the unknown will happen.

   When traffic piles up, the microphone doesn't work, and you must speak in two minutes, four people have questions in the last two minutes of your meeting, or your daughter calls at 6:00 a.m. with an emergency, you can behave knowing you have been expecting these unknown unknowns. This doesn't mean you have to plan to infinity. You can learn to accept that the unknown will occur.

2. Before my dad died, my parents would pop over to our house when they were in the area. We didn't know when their visits would occur, and they didn't inform us ahead of time. When I worked from home, even before the pandemic, they always seemed to come over when I was on a conference call, talking to physicians, running a workshop, or working on a deadline. My parents coming

over was a known unknown. We knew it could happen. We didn't know when. I couldn't stop my meetings or workshops.

The first time my parents popped over, I was annoyed. I couldn't spend time with them. It seemed they thought I was available at a moment's notice because I worked from home. My parents stopping by our house in the middle of the workweek became my known unknown.

Our plan was that my husband could stop what he was doing in most cases to attend to my parents, and I would visit with my parents only if I could. I also spoke kind words to myself if I couldn't attend to my parents. I placed no expectations on myself *to do it all.* I did what I could and was happy about it. You can try the same.

3. The first time I listened to my taped voice recording, I cringed. When I became a coach, others encouraged me to listen to my coaching conversations and to build a practice of listening to myself coach. Listening to myself was awkward, and the best thing I did to grow my coaching skills.

I made a point of doing things making me uncomfortable. I made a point to do one thing a day, terrifying me. If I could avoid meeting or talking to others, I would feel my life complete. Strangers, strange situations, and unfamiliar places make me uncomfortable.

I began pushing myself to new levels of discomfort. Given that I have spoken at TEDx events and run global workshops, I would say playing with risk has worked for me. Here are a few of the things I began doing:

a. I joined a group where I didn't know a single person
b. I volunteered for a board of director role in an organization
c. I wrote a post on LinkedIn
d. I wrote a blog article
e. I commented on a stranger's post
f. I recorded myself on camera
g. I posted a recording of myself
h. I (gasp) introduced myself to strangers
i. I talked in front of audiences where I knew no one

4. About 5 percent of women are professional poker players (Sofen 2022). For some reason, women do not flock to this game. There is not a single poker champion not having lost a few hands on their rise into the Poker Hall of Fame. Winning goes with losing.

Jennifer Harman, one of three women in the Poker Hall of Fame, says of her poise, "nothing fazes me (Barnes 2021)." I'm not saying you have to start playing poker. I suggest you improve your risk muscle and get comfortable letting nothing faze you.

THE POISE-PRESENCE OVERLAP
I would argue that the executive assistant is the most influential person in any company. This person has the power to add your topic to the schedule, ensure you are seated, or your reservations are made in a way most advantageous for your

growth or can help to stonewall you. Nevertheless, the executive assistant is the least powerful persona in the C-suite, according to many.

Someone with a poise-presence overlap may be missing power. A substantial poise-presence overlap suggests you might not speak up when you should or speak too much about nothing. At times in my life, I've had a solid poise-presence overlap and lacked power. I talked much, almost dancing around what I wanted to say, in the end, I didn't even know my point. I was trying to cover up my meaning by adding more words to the mix instead of saying what I thought. People walked away, confused, wondering what I was trying to say. The sad part is that I walked away confused. The other side to this situation is that you might not speak up when you really should. Both of these may happen when your power needs strengthening.

YOUR POWER ROLODEX

If power is your missing or fragile component, I suggest adding power to your Rolodex. A Rolodex is a rotating file device whose sole purpose is to contain business contact information at the ready and easily accessible.

Here are a few suggestions:

- Flip the Rolodex and remove the obstacle. When I speak in circles, I might ask myself, "What's getting in your way from speaking clearly," and I might respond, "I'm worried about what others will think of me." Remove the obstacle with "What would you be doing if you weren't worried about what others thought of you?" I discovered I could state my point and sit in powerful quiet if I didn't care about others' opinions. Powerful quiet, I've found, can unnerve even the most powerful in the room.

- Add power to your Rolodex. In any situation, you can imagine you are the CEO or the person in authority. What would you do or say about your challenge if you were the CEO, the lead, the head doctor, the department chair, or whatever is the seat of power in your situation?

When your characteristics are imbalanced, either too much or too little compared to other traits, you may feel the imbalance. I felt imbalanced and powerless when my parents came over. I felt exhausted because I couldn't be with them. There is a way you can use your biomarkers to help your energy efficiency. You can use what you've learned to avoid the energy suck and instead channel the renewing energy efficiency from being in your authentic leadership zone.

THE ENERGY SUCK

You know what the energy suck is. Meetings. The one person on your team, the tactical team member, identifying tactics when you are reviewing strategy, the people in the discussion taking up the airtime and saying nothing of consequence to the meeting's purpose, or meetings droning on with no outcome. What is your energy suck?

What drains your energy quicker than those electrical bug zappers draining bugs of life? What is the thing dragging you down? Stop and make a note of it. Make a note of all of them.

The thing zapping your energy and draining you of life, similar to an electrical bug zapper, isn't the thing you believe it is. It isn't the person taking up valuable airtime in the meeting. It isn't covering the same thing for the fifth time with the same person. It isn't what you think it is. Whatever you wrote down or pondered, not it.

The energy suck happens when you operate outside your power, poise, and presence zone. What is the zone? Your power, poise, and presence zone is where all three, power, poise, and presence, overlap, your authentic leadership.

THE ZONE

If you envision power, poise, and presence being three concentric circles, the zone is where all three overlap, what we've identified being your concentrated authentic leadership. In this zone, you are on fire. You have presence, poise, and power in this zone. Nothing gets in your way when you are in the zone. You rock-n-roll in this zone, and you know all will go well. In *Harry Potter* speak, this is the Felix Felicis potion (Rowling 2015). Felix Felicis is a potion of liquid luck. This potion makes the drinker lucky for some time. Everything the subject tries while under the influence of Felix Felicis is a success, even if seeming a failure at the time. You have your own Felix Felicis, your authentic leadership zone. Operate in this zone, expand this zone and your day can be productive and life-giving, even regenerative.

In my experience, when you work with your authentic and natural talents in your authentic leadership space of power, poise, and presence, you consume less energy; you regenerate while you are in this space, and you can emerge with more ending energy than your starting point. Imagine driving a solar-powered car that fully refuels from the sun while driving, and this is a perfect analogy for what this area is.

Figure 3. Graphical representation of your energy efficient, authentic leadership space showing your concentrated authentic leadership zone.

THE SUCK

Everything outside the power, poise, and presence circles is the suck. You have half a tank of gas. Every stop-and-go action consumes more gas, and the price of refueling rises while driving. Is the person consuming valuable airtime in a meeting by saying nothing and leaving you no time to address your agenda item the suck? Nope, at least not in my experience. Airtime eater is not your energy drain. The suck happens when you violate your authentic leadership values. What does violating your values mean? Let me give you a client example.

Jan, an up-and-coming VP and high performer, was stuck in a group of mediocre performers talking around items, ending meetings with no progress or actions because time ran out. Jan had no time to get to her agenda items because the meeting wandered out of time. Jan values clear and consistent communication. If she were operating out of her authentic leadership, she could interrupt, summarize the findings, and ask for a direct one-line takeaway to conclude the wandering. She sat frustrated. The meeting was sailing without any heading. The meeting ended without any conclusions. Jan concluded the meeting was useless. At least she had a conclusion.

In my experience, the drain happens because we violate our authentic leadership. We struggle and battle not to do what we want to happen because we are waiting for someone else to do it. The back-and-forth struggle takes copious amounts of energy. No wonder you feel drained. You are the one for whom you've been waiting. It's always been you. Listen to your power, poise, and presence, and act from your authentic leadership. Listen to your authentic leadership and trust.

Jan refused to step into her power during the meeting. What was getting in Jan's way was fear. Fear was her suck. Jan spoke up in the next meeting and regained her energy and some energy for others in the group meeting. She found her authentic leadership.

The energy suck, as Jan discovered, is from fighting against what would make things better. *You.*

Figure 4. Graphical representation of the suck space, everything residing outside of your authentic leadership space.

GETTING BACK IN THE ZONE

What does it mean for you to get back into the zone? For Jan, it was realizing she could interrupt, summarize the findings, and ask for a direct one-line takeaway. She realized thinking she could do this, simply thinking this way, not doing anything, alone gave her energy. She realized that if she were operating from her authentic leadership zone, full of power, poise, and presence, she would interrupt and summarize in a heartbeat. Jan thought her struggle was with the others. She struggled with herself, not with her colleagues, droning on directionless.

Embrace the suck. Examine it. What do you think is responsible for your energy drain? What parts of your power, poise, and presence are you not honoring? Answer this question, and you'll be closer to returning to your zone.

Let your authentic leadership embrace the suck. Leaning into your characteristic traits and embracing them may mean confrontation, challenge, and adopting a new solution.

CHAPTER FOURTEEN

Memorials

———

The world breaks everyone and afterward many are strong at the broken places.

—ERNEST HEMINGWAY

IN MEMORIAL

"Artificial intelligence (AI) is helping physicians decide what might be the best treatment per patient. Gone are the days when we prescribe the same treatment for the same disease to different patients. AI is shaking up patient care. We personalize care with a patient-centered approach, a unique treatment based on the patient's biomarkers, genetic markers, or history. AI is even changing how we train medical students. Virtual patients give students real-world skills."

The speaker's early morning lecture mesmerized me. I hadn't even taken a sip of my coffee. His talk hooked us. When he wrapped up by sharing a memorial to his mentor, a victim of cancer, we followed our pied piper.

Choking back tears, he shared how his colleague inspired, motivated, and helped him be a doctor and scientist. He shared his heartfelt pain at losing his colleague. She lost her cancer health care battle. He had us wiping away tears.

He gushed at how she had impacted him. "She is the reason for my success. She showed how I could be a physician and a scientist and do it with grace even while dying," he said. His memorial at the close of a remarkable presentation honored her. Commendable and admirable.

The memorial, however, taught me a lesson. It shook me and challenged me. I asked myself, "How can I honor those in my life?" Indeed, how can you honor those remarkable women, men, and anyone contributing to your growth and development both in death and in life?

Memorials are laudable. However, we often miss momentary opportunities to validate, boost, and give gratitude to those deserving individuals in our lives. Their burgeoning leadership is waiting for your affirmation.

Please don't wait until they've passed on to tell the world what an inspiration they have been for you and how they helped you. Giving someone public praise doesn't require a doctor's certificate, a CEO role, or being a leader. You can give thanks or praise in a mention in a presentation, in an email to a group, or at an event. Strengthen your credit by giving tangible examples of what the person did for you. Please don't wait until they are gone before you let others know how they impacted you.

OPPORTUNITIES

Using the conference example and taking the concept of a memorial, you can turn an opportunity of giving thanks into a living memorial. When giving presentations, trainees, emerging leaders, and even seasoned leaders share their work broadly. These persons can take the opportunity to thank their supporters and add context to those words of thanks.

CONTEXT

Providing context gives color and depth to the support provided. Women are less prone to self-promote their work. Non-leaders are essential in sharing actionable input and context. This information provides leaders and others with eyes in the back of their heads—your perspective on what others do matters.

Different people provide varying types of support to others. Certain people supporting others may have less to demonstrate in tangible deliverables. You are their tangible deliverable. The McKinsey data suggests that women in the workplace play a huge role in supporting others (Burns 2021). If she boosts you or your work, your feedback role is vital. You have the power to spread her reach, to help in her promotion, and to help others see her for what she has done for you. Spreading your colleagues' achievements raises their impact factor with leadership and provides concrete examples of their management and leadership capacity by demonstrating the tangibles you have provided.

When providing context, tell what the person did, the conditions of the person's input, and what sacrifices they made to boost your work. When deciding what to include, ask yourself what would have happened had the person not been there to support you. Here are a few examples of how you might explore this skill:

- "I couldn't have completed this work without Lindsay's assistance. She gave her time and expertise to ensure I had the proper safety factors. Had she not been there, we would have had a different discussion. She helped me see potential pitfalls and helped me address them before they became more significant issues."

- "I wish to thank Ed. He gave his time and stayed late to ensure I addressed the right quality needs, and he did this at risk to his workload without a complaint. Without him, I could not have completed this work with high quality. He fosters a supportive environment ensuring our organization is more effective."

- "Through Olivia's confident display of knowledge and her direct feedback, I was confident when I didn't think it would be possible. I spoke up and stopped a problem from making its way into the product. I couldn't have done this without her."

TANGIBLES

Research shows that women get less direct and actionable feedback in their performance reviews. They aren't the only ones (Doldor 2019). Often, leaders aren't in the role to see their people's tangible goods; instead, third-party feedback or hearsay influences them. Leaders cannot often observe first-hand what their direct reports are doing and rely on second or third-party feedback. When giving feedback, different people respond to different types of feedback. Due to their leadership roles, leaders may not be working side by side with everyone on their team. Good leaders know how to manage their people. They understand how to influence each person in a way resonating with the person and provide feedback where most often, they don't have first-party knowledge. Leadership is challenging and also rewarding when you lead from the zone.

You can help your leaders by providing actionable and direct examples of others' leadership qualities. This feedback lets leaders see the things they don't know, and it also lets them know what the person is doing to make their performance shine. Providing leadership with actionable feedback demonstrates your capacity to acknowledge and give input on concrete performance, a skill necessary for career growth.

Identifying tangible acts is an easy thing to do. However, assuming everybody has the same knowledge may get in your way. Does everybody know this?

Identify the tangible activity the person did.

In graduate school, my mentor suffered from small-cell lung carcinoma. While being treated, his coprincipal investigator became my surrogate mentor. Lilach ran through my manuscripts with detailed feedback making my written products shine. Her exquisite attention to detail astounded me. She had her lab, funding, and projects to run. She would correct my sentence structure and grammar by using what I had provided and reorganizing my document to make accepting the changes easy for me.

To this day, I have no idea how she could rearrange my sentence structure with a single-tracked change. When I try to replicate what she did, I have at least three tracked types of changes. Her modifications were clean. It made the editing process simple.

Her tangible activity: Exquisite editing of my manuscript.

Her impact: She taught me how to refine my writing and elevate my manuscripts, and taught me by example how to promote others' work.

PROVIDING PRAISE

Doling out contextual praise and noticing positive contributions people make can be a difficult task for some. Giving praise is easy. I find those easy praises are cheers, lacking the punch of added context for meaningful praise. What does giving praise mean to you? Is your praise a compliment or a cheer similar to "Thanks for a job well done?" There is nothing wrong with a job well done. The statement lacks context and tangible praise. Giving praise or feedback takes practice, and many of us are out of practice.

Giving praise is hard work. Feedback is essential, not simply for the person involved. For the organization and yourself to grow, feedback is paramount. I have a view. You have a view. They are both different. We have views of others, a view the other doesn't have. You know things. Certain things you share with others, and certain things you don't. Collectively, this is a Johari window (Luft 1961).

Johari Window

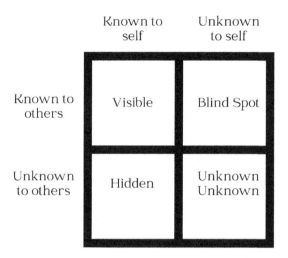

Figure 1. A Johari window describing what is known to you, unknown to you, known to others, and unknown to others.

A Johari window describes four different views of self. The quadrant of knowledge known to the person of interest and known to others is the visible quadrant. This is what is visible or known to others. What you hide from others is what you know. Others don't know what you are hiding. Your blind spot is the area others see or experience and you aren't aware exists. The things you don't know, you don't know, and others don't know land in the unknown quadrant. Feedback can help others see their blind spots. When you give feedback, consider the following:

- What makes this person different from others?
- What makes this person unique?
- How does their activity make the organization stronger?
- What comes easy for this person to do?
- What one thing could they do to improve themselves or how they operate?

GIVING THANKS

Not everyone is comfortable telling or receiving praise. Women are rare to praise their work (Burns 2021). Two-thirds of women are uncomfortable praising their efforts. Pointing out accomplishments helps reveal what others don't know and can help people overcome obstacles in pointing out their work to others. Remember, you are always leading people by your example. I pick on women. However, women aren't alone in refraining from praising their work. In your ordinary course of activities, you can be intentional in sharing your accomplishments and in giving thanks or praise.

When giving thanks, a simple model to use can be the following:

- Provide context
- Provide public praise
- Share the tangibles

Providing public praise may seem daunting. The important part is that the praise is more than "thanks." The praise doesn't require a speech. You could state your thanks for what they did and how it helped you. Nothing more. Silence after a well-timed thankful statement can allow the significance of your saying to settle and reverberate. The benefit of this technique is that anyone can do this. You don't need a leadership role to give praise and have the praise make an impact. You can be a trainee and praise with this three-step technique.

CHAPTER FIFTEEN

Creating a Powerfully Poised and Present Culture

No matter what culture, everywhere around the world, people get together to eat.

—GUY FIERI

You have learned fantastic superpowers, principles, and techniques. You might be excited to share your learnings with others. In this chapter, we'll explore ways you can share your newfound insights through modeling, inviting, celebrating, and we'll even map out a few things to avoid when sharing power, poise, and presence with others.

MODEL IT

A powerful way to encourage authentic leadership in others is to model it. Acknowledging I am modeling power, poise, and presence for others invites my behavior to a higher standard, which is not easy. Modeling authentic leadership, however, is rewarding. I tend to behave differently when I know all eyes are on me. I am more deliberate when I am modeling a behavior.

A few years back, a friend asked me to be her sponsor at church. Welcoming people into our church community involved pairing the new person with a sponsor. A sponsor is someone walking with the person along the path into the church. A sponsor witnesses the candidate's journey into the church. The sponsor lifts the candidate in prayer and helps the candidate discover the church, a living practice, and a day-to-day reality.

When I became someone's sponsor, I lived under the name of a Christian. I doubt anyone would have accused me of acting like one. I was in the middle of searching for my truth when my friend approached me to be her sponsor. Wanting to help my friend, I said yes, not realizing what my yes entailed.

I was her role model. "Uh-oh," I thought, and I also told myself, "If I am going to model the behaviors for her, then I want to model the behavior correctly." I sought knowledge, prayer, and sacraments, and something authentic met me in the seeking. I found what I did not have when she approached me to be her sponsor. I found the lived reality of the divine. By modeling the behaviors, I sought to demonstrate. I discovered myself transforming. I wasn't faking it. I was trying to understand how to express my faith authentically. When you model power, poise, and presence for others, your modeling can lead to your transformation.

Modeling your authentic leadership will convey your power, poise, and presence style, and others will see an example in you. You will encourage others in simple ways through your lived example. Your example doesn't need to model perfection. You give a real example. Faking it until you make it is an approach, helpful when nothing else works for you. The fake method won't fake others or yourself. To convince yourself and others, be your version of reality. Your version leads to authentic admiration, meaning others will attempt to possess what you are modeling. Your version may be messy. Your attempt is genuine and admirable. A fake version lacks authenticity.

INVITE OTHERS
You become powerful by giving power away.

Have you ever learned something and were eager to share your learnings to discover no one wanted to know what you learned? While you're practicing and learning power, poise, and presence, hesitate the urge to tell others. In the natural course of modeling your authentic leadership, people will notice and come to admire your supernatural ability to remain powerful, poised, and present. They will want to know how you manage your composure, your cue inviting them to discover authentic leadership for themselves. If this book helps you, then, by all means, I invite you to share the book with others. The book's structure helps craft and ease the practice of your authentic leadership with power, poise, and presence.

A self-assessment starting point can reveal skill gaps. The assessments can be a tool to invite others to discover their brand of authentic leadership, followed by an invitation to find a small way to develop and explore biomarkers. This book is an excellent starting point for those looking to cultivate power, poise, and presence in their own lives. To advance in the practice of authentic leadership, I invite you to work with a certified executive coach to take you further and uncover how to address your challenges with your unique gifts.

CELEBRATE POWER, POISE, AND PRESENCE MOMENTS

Celebrating power, poise, and presence moments is a way to encourage and invite others to build a powerful, poised, and present culture. Celebrating authentic leadership requires effort on your part. However, it requires less effort than modeling requires. Make a habit of noticing power, poise, and presence moments. Point these moments out and help others celebrate these moments. You may be helping someone discover their blind spot!

Often, we are unaware of our strengths. My son doesn't enjoy doing jigsaw puzzles. When we spent our winter evenings in Minnesota working on a jigsaw puzzle, he would do something else. We gathered around the puzzle for an hour after dinner. He would walk by and, with casual flair, pick up a piece, snap it into place, and walk away. We would stop and gaze at the seven-year-old. He didn't even realize his gift for seeing through the complex with simplicity.

When you use your strengths, you leave others flabbergasted. Like my son, most of us walk around unaware that we possess a rare gift. My son assumes everyone could do what he did: see through the complicated with simplicity. Each of our gifts is different. Celebrate these moments when you see them.

It's your responsibility to point out and celebrate unique gifts and skills to others when you see them. When you observe a power, poise, or presence moment or any gift-filled moment, celebrate it. Chances are that the person demonstrating a superpower isn't aware they possess a gift. The celebration here doesn't mean you need to call for a party. Pointing it out is all you need to do.

For example,
"Your composure under pressure is amazing. Have you always been able to be calm?"

"Your confidence in the team helps us get the project completed. Thanks."

The model is straightforward:
1. Notice the biomarker, characteristic, or attribute you witnessed.
2. Say what you observed.
3. Tell what impact you observed.
4. A word of thanks (optional).

WHAT NOT TO DO

Don't be intrusive when creating power, poise, and presence for others.

DON'T TELL

Does telling others appeal to you? If you like to tell others, consider this: By telling someone what to do to step into their power, poise, or presence, you might rob them of the gift of learning it on their own. I've found that telling others what to do is the slowest path toward progress. Telling robs someone of their creative resources and drives them away from the direction you want them to take. Unless you've been asked, you're running out of time, or it's an emergency, telling someone to do anything is like taking a slow detour landing you somewhere you didn't want to explore.

My dad had this habit of inhaling a swift, deep breath through clenched teeth and holding his forehead when trying to control his reaction to someone he'd dubbed a know-it-all. He'd also utter under his breath in Spanish, *nosy*. He hated having someone telling him how to do things when he hadn't asked for someone's input. Nosy was anyone telling him how to do something. Anytime someone told him how to do anything, he'd call them *nosy* and would disregard what others told him even if what *nosy* said was right.

What mattered to him was that *nosy* irritated him. He did not like *nosy*, this person telling him how to do things.

Don't be nosy. Be a partner. Help the people in your life think. Help them discover. If you do opt to say anything, tell what worked for you and invite the other person to find out what might work for them.

One of the biggest reasons I hear given for telling instead of partnering with someone is "it's faster if I tell them."

I ask my clients, "What's faster?"

My clients discover they can say something fast. The change, however, is slow on the uptake. If you want to go fast, you must pass through *slow* on your way there. Even the Ferrari starts at zero mph/kph.

It's faster to go slow and help others discover. Going slow also encourages people to let the behavior emerge and encourages better rooting, allowing the behavior to transform into a habit.

Slow down—partner up. Discover together.

DON'T DEMAND

You become powerful by giving power away to others, letting them accept or reject what you give. People have a wealth of lived experiences. Demanding they should use yours is short-sighted. They don't have your lived embodied experience. You have yours, not theirs. You don't know what power, poise, or confidence looks like for someone else.

Avoid using terms like *you should* or *you need to* and instead, help the people in your life discover their authentic leadership for themselves. Invite them. Share the book. An invitation is open for acceptance or rejection. Learn to take both.

DON'T LECTURE

How far you go in life depends on your being tender with the young, compassionate with the aged, sympathetic with the striving, and tolerant of the weak and the strong.
Because someday in your life you will have been all of these.

—GEORGE WASHINGTON CARVER

Be quick to compassion and slow to criticize. Chances are, if someone did something wrong, they are more aware of their miss than you are. Find something to relate to in their challenge. If you are thinking of pointing out facts to them, understand that facts don't change minds. People change when others make them feel good regarding the change (Boyatzis 2019).

Leave the lectures for the lecture hall.

CHAPTER SIXTEEN

Raising Powerfully Poised and Present Children

———

To remain a joyful family requires much from both the parents and the children. Each member of the family has to become, in a special way, the servant of the others.

—JOHN PAUL II

Raising powerful, poised, and present children requires much of parents and requires much of children. While children may not need to exude leadership presence in their third-grade math class, they can benefit from having the foundation ready. This is what childhood is about, laying the foundation for future skills and habits, and creating a lifetime of opportunities. Raising powerful, poised, and present children is the work of parents and us all. This chapter will give you many ideas and suggestions for helping children grow into powerful, poised, and present adults.

GROW STRONGER

The Poise chapter introduced how my family created resilient children by responding to cries of help with helpful advice. This concept can help you to raise powerful, poised, and present children.

BECOME YOUR CHILD'S ALLY

An ally partners with another for mutual benefit. A cheerleader offers vocal support. An ally comes next to someone to partner with them and joins them right where they are. You don't have to pick up their struggle or challenge. Help them work out problems or challenges by being their thought partner.

Struggling stings, and the sting is not nasty when you can share the burden with a partner. A partner shares the responsibility by seeking to understand. What is making this a challenge for them? Trying to understand what is making their struggle a challenge is empathy. You can be a true partner by sharing your struggles. Being a parent doesn't mean you can't be vulnerable.

Vulnerability is not complete transparency and disclosure (Brown 2018). Through moments of empathy, we can measure vulnerability. For example, "That stinks. I've been there, and it can seem overwhelming."

My husband's Irish way of saying, "This stinks. I've been there" is "Grow stronger." What's your "grow stronger" call to action?

FAILURE IS PART OF SUCCESS

I wish I learned to accept failure as part of the formula for success. I wasn't. I learned humiliation. I learned to be ashamed of failure. I became failure. My future became strewn with rich failure moments. I discovered along the way that failure is rich with data. Failure is a phenomenon producing rich data. We can't purchase failure data from the store or from others.

A mollusk responds to an irritant by producing nacre, a substance reducing the irritation. The nacre builds up and contributes to creating a shiny, beautiful pearl. Matured failure is a pearl. For the mollusk, they have to experience the irritant. Otherwise, no pearl. You can wish for success all you want. If you don't share the annoyance of failure, you won't have the data you need to make success. I had to rewire myself to milk failure for all its worth. Failure was worth even more than I realized it could be. Failure is priceless. Failure gives me something success can never deliver.

Success says, "Yes, you did it!" Success doesn't answer the question, "What made it a success?" Failure answers with definitive knowledge the question of what doesn't work, meaning we can eliminate failure. The answer to "what didn't work" is priceless because it provides a treasure trove of small steps paving the road to measurable, repeatable, and sustainable success. Failure isn't the enemy. Failure is my good friend because he gives me something success never can. Success makes me feel great. Failure makes me great. Failure gives me opportunities and varied pathways to success. The journey to success becomes an adventure of risk, reward, and opportunity. The rewards are the seeds of success, learning opportunities, and ways to play with the success. Success alone cannot provide failure data.

I suggest you help your children embrace failure like a playground, meaning you, the parent, can help model what handling failure looks like. They are always watching you and on the constant learning patrol, seeking what they might learn from you. When dinner fails, your boss is a jerk and leaves you out to dry, you're working someplace you hate or any other failure in your life, ask yourself:

- What is this moment teaching me?
- What am I learning?
- What opportunities are here for me in failure?
- What am I teaching by my actions and reactions?

Opportunities lie on all sides of an outcome, success, failure, and even when it's a draw. Failure gives you more opportunities to learn. Success gives few. Failure provides abundant data and exceptional opportunities. Don't waste your failure gems. Teach your children to expand their vision beyond failure. The failure data has something to give you, something to teach you. We often throw it out with the rubbish. If you are throwing out failure with the trash, know you are teaching your children to throw out failure with the trash. Go searching for the pearls in the garbage. Pearls are sitting there waiting for discovery. How many pearls have you thrown away over your lifetime, and how many more will you be throwing out from this day forward?

EAT WORMS

When our daughter came home from school complaining that a kid didn't like her, her Papa would start singing. He refuses to sing in church. If he's making fun of something, he'll be singing a tune in no time. He'd regale her with the lament of how nobody liked her and how she should go eat worms.

She'd beg him to stop. Hearing about eating worms was worse than any treatment she got at school. Maybe kids didn't like her. Maybe they did. His point was that you could be sorry for yourself, believe you are unlovable despite all the evidence to the contrary, all the way to the end of wherever the sad song takes you, or choose a different story.

I'm happy to report that she avoided eating worms, and if someone doesn't like her, she will continue to be herself in her own story and to her tune. You don't need to tell your kids to eat worms. What I'll suggest is for you to be you and build up their resiliency.

This can be the hardest thing for a parent to do. Parents rescue and protect kids. Rescuing and protecting are part of our job and can impede our ability to build their resiliency. If your child is in danger, someone is bullying them, or is in over their head, you must rescue them. If they are uncomfortable, you could choose to be their thought partner, their ally. How you parent is your choice. I'll provide you with some resiliency-building options. You decide if they are something you'd like to consider for your practice.

RESCUE RESILIENCY MODEL

In case you are rescuing, it's worth noting that you can build their resiliency while saving and protecting them. One resilient model would be to:

1. Affirm
2. Clarify your role
3. Act/set expectations
4. Reaffirm

Affirmation might sound like this:

"This is a difficult spot for someone in third grade. I'm not sure many adults would handle this as well as you are."

Clarifying your role might sound like this:

"You know what? This is a safety issue. I must step in, and I'll need your help. The bottom line is this affects you. You should have a role in resolving it."

Acting/setting expectations might sound like this:

"Today, I will call the principal, and tomorrow we will discuss it together. My end goal is to help you resolve this. You can step back in and lead yourself as you have before. What do you think?"

Reaffirming might sound like this:

"It's a wise person knowing when to seek help. Thank you for coming to me and allowing me to be your helper."

In this model, you are affirming their leadership capacity. You are clarifying what you will seek to do for both of you, and you are explaining where the boundaries lie for you and your child. You also affirm their role in the situation, allowing them to see your role and their role.

SOME THINGS TO CONSIDER

Consider involving your child in the process. Ask for their input and let them be part of the decision-making. Their wisdom may surprise you. At some stage in your parenting journey, you may find success when you step aside from being a rescuer to being their advocate. An invested rescuer can feel deep emotion in regard to an outcome. An advocate is uninvested with emotion in their work and won't seek to do what will make the child comfortable. As a result, an advocate has the distance to see and be present with dispassion. When you can advocate in this way, you may find a variety of options available.

A STANDARD RESILIENCY MODEL

If you aren't in a crisis or in rescuing mode, another resiliency scenario to try would be to

1. Invite
2. Partner for Success
3. Discover
4. Step
5. Affirm

INVITATION

Extend an invitation to partner for success. An invitation implies a response. A response can be a negative response or a positive one. If they reject your help, then respect it. This applies as well if you know the solution to their problem. This step is crucial for building trust. If the answer is no, drop it like a hot potato. Leave the door open for them to walk through if and when they want. For example, "Okay, the offer will stay open if you change your mind later."

The invitation doesn't have to be on paper. It can be a casual invitation. For example, "I'd be happy to help you think through it together. We might find a different way for you to approach this. What do you think?"

PARTNER FOR SUCCESS

If you know the solution to their problem, put it in a box, label it for delivery to the bottom of the ocean, and send it. Once you do, you are almost ready to partner with someone for success. Maybe no one picked your child for the team again. Perhaps they ate their way through a bowl of cookie dough. Maybe they failed a test, and they feel like a failure. You aren't problem-solving. You are building resiliency.

To build strong resiliency, help them discover what they want. If no one picked them for the team, and you think your child has two left feet, their hand-eye coordination is suspect, and you believe they'll never make the team, set your beliefs aside. What you think doesn't matter. This is their dream. Hold their vision for them and take it further by asking, for example, "What would you be doing if they picked you for the team?" Help them discover their future.

Paint a clear vision of success, including what they feel, what skills they have, what's happening, and who is around them. If the team selects them, perhaps they practice for several hours a day. They might comment on things they are giving up to be on the team or say they are making friends and winning games.

DISCOVER

In the discovery phase, you stick to their goal and help them uncover various ways to get from where they are to where they want to be. All you have to do is ask questions and be curious. They will discover.

By partnering with your child to help them craft their vision, you are doing important work in assisting them to clarify what their success looks like. Suppose your child says what they are doing in the future is hanging out, making friends with people on the team, and winning games. You might offer a challenge, for example: "It seems like you'd rather have this feeling of success and friends. You didn't say much about the work going into being on a team. Practice takes up a lot of time, and you'll have to give up something. What do you think?"

They might recognize that what they want isn't to be on the team. Instead, they want to have a group of friends. There are plenty of ways to create a couple of friends. One way is to be on a team. Being on a team is not the only way to have friends. There is no guarantee that being on a team brings you friends. You might offer them some help to brainstorm a few ways to feel successful and have friends and let them choose what they want to do or not do.

STEP

Once you've outlined several possibilities, you help them outline one step toward their goal. Help them address how they are going to get past any challenges. Perhaps your child is determined to make a few friends, or maybe they are committed to practicing daily for twenty minutes to build up their skills. You might ask, "How are you going to make sure you stick to your plan to practice every day?" or "What's going to happen when you miss a day?"

Your goal, as a partner, is to help them think through their step to ensure it's healthy and help them figure out how they plan to stick to the next step they are planning to take.

AFFIRM

This affirmation step is similar to the one in the previous model. You are building their resiliency and agency to grow amid challenges and not sink. Notice how they've grown and let them know. For example, you might say, "You have a good plan, something you didn't have earlier. It looks like you are ready to put it to work. You did some good work in putting a plan together! Thanks for letting me help you."

By helping them craft their plan, you are building their power to affect their situation. You are helping them build resiliency and how to tackle problems and manage discomfort when they don't know their solution. You are also helping them engage confidently in their future and develop their presence.

TEMPER TANTRUMS

You might wonder how to handle temper tantrums with power, poise, and presence. Is that even possible?

At a very early age, we refused to honor temper tantrums. I remember my husband telling our son at nine months of age, "Don't show me your baby temper," and he'd put him in his crib for a baby time-out.

Tantrums are full of emotions. To address tantrums, you may want to be emotionally distant or dispassionate to avoid absorbing the emotions onto yourself. It's their tantrum, not yours. Help them deal with their emotions. Emotional outbursts from children or adults are clues about something they can't or don't know how to say.

A child doesn't know what they need, and if they are in tantrum mode, they need fewer options, not more. They may need a nap, and the only way they know how to say it is by yelling, screaming, and maniacally running around. If you are in public, this can be awkward. Remember, emotions are like waves. You might be at the peak of their emotional tantrum.

A scientist would isolate the specimen, observe it, and draw conclusions. The specimen will tire itself out and eventually rest. Let's assume the specimen is not tiring themselves out and are instead being violent, slapping, hitting, or biting.

Scientists working with violent reactive substances suit up for the occasion or use quarantine measures. I never needed to quarantine my child but was prepared to do so if a violent outburst occurred.

A few suggestions for dealing with a temper tantrum with power, poise, and presence follow:

Reduce their stimulation. At the peak of a tantrum, a child or an adult cannot handle anything more. Distracting them with shows, games, or toys can worsen the situation.

Eliminate or reduce their options. Do not provide them with options. They are not able to process options until they are past the tantrum.

Isolate if necessary and do not tolerate violence.

Infect them with powerful silence. Embrace powerful silence. Tantrums are seeking interaction. Interacting with tantrums strengthens them. Powerful silence and calm can disarm tantrums, perhaps through emotional contagion. Be prepared for a long stretch of silence. At the very least, you will stay calm.

Parenting is a demanding job. Fortunately, the skills you are building as a parent can apply to the workplace. Even if you aren't a parent, you can shape and use these models and suggestions in the workplace to create a powerfully poised and present culture.

Afterword

——

Life, it turns out, is infinitely more clever and adaptable than anyone had ever supposed.

—ARTHUR CONAN DOYLE

THE FIRE

One of my lifetime's most incredible lows, burning down a house by following the leadership of someone undeserving of my following, started my journey toward uncovering the source of authentic leadership. When my father saw the fire, he knew the fire department was on the way. He also knew the family next door were immigrants with nothing except their livelihood, family, and house. Our family had nothing except the work of his hands to rely upon for income. Not knowing what might happen, he said nothing and risked everything to walk with firm purpose straight into the heart of flames to rescue lives and our neighborhood. It would baffle him if you had asked him if he had power, poise, or presence then or ever.

He didn't realize I was watching and learning. You probably aren't aware that others are watching you, learning from you, and will later model what they see you do. The future rests in your powerfully poised and present hands.

WHAT'S MISSING

I deliberately didn't discuss dress or attire in addressing authentic leadership. While dress and attire are important components for anyone, authentic leadership involves more important items than your wardrobe. Clothes certainly have the potential to make us feel or feel seen a certain way. Feeling seen a certain way doesn't mean we know the way. What should be memorable about you to others is you and not your dress, attire, jewelry, shoes, or wardrobe.

THE LESSON

I hope sharing my curious journey into healthcare and leadership helps you gently lead in the most harmonious way for yourself. I hope you take this method, practice authentic leadership, and teach it to others to help create a world where authentic leadership is the norm and where power, poise, and presence are starting points for everyone instead of a destination.

Go be brilliant!

Lizette Warner
lizette@optimumvobis.com

Find additional resources at www.lizettewarner.com.

Acknowledgments

I am powerfully grateful to my husband, Shawn. He's always put me first without question. While he was writing and publishing his first book, *Leigh Howard and the Ghosts of Simmons-Pierce Manor*, he encouraged me to tell my story, spent his time helping me revise my manuscript, dealt with my writing and deadline tantrums, and helped me refine my thoughts with his psychology and social work expertise.

My clients and coach partners encouraged me to write a book, sometimes presuming I already wrote one. Thank you to Shallyn Williams, who asked me before I had even considered writing a book, "When's your book coming out, Lizette?"

I am grateful to all my powerful clients, present and past, whose names and roles I changed to protect their identities in the narrative of *Power, Poise, and Presence.*

If you have ever written a book, you know the dedication needed for and the revising and editing involved to elevate your work. Writing a book involves a team. I am indebted to my beta readers and thought partners, who encouraged me and read the early and late versions of my manuscript. Anytime I asked for assistance, Pam Aks, PCC, the most energetic, positive force I have ever known, eagerly hopped on my book train as I was scurrying from carriage to carriage during the revisions process. Donna Whitcomb and Amy Gilchrist hopped aboard my train to give comments on my early drafts.

I am indebted to my choir sister, Debbie Thomson, RN, for her medical expertise and contribution to my book. I appreciate Dr. Sannamari Kotaluoto for her medical expertise and for ensuring my Finnish language usage was correct.

My author community stuck by me as I marched toward my finish line. My author community included my Philips colleagues (past and present), chief members, ICF supporters, F1C coaches and family, friends, and clients.

I'm grateful to all my Philips author community supporters: Donna Whitcomb, Lori Medugno, Brian Welch, Julie Brodowski, Wendy Hopkins, Susan Szanyi, Dana Senik-Puckett, Derek Rose, Alex Dresner, Donna Stolz, Laura Visconti, Donna Weber, Jody Rofelson, Nira Mahesh, Riva Ille, Jenn Smith, Paul Redder, Lorna Dewhirt, Carrie Shaw, Dhruv Jhoti, Katherine Freedman, Erin MacMillan, Michelle Avery, Kimberly Graftenreed, Lindsay Peightel, Afifa Scognamiglio, and Stacey Salazar.

I appreciate my chief author community supporters: Jennifer Howlett, Jenny Bauleke, Angela Piner, Danielle Chandler, Varsha Chandramouli, Anne Marie Watkins, Casey Carpenter, Dee Kane, Pooja Tejwani, Wendy Balow, Tanya

Rose, Jennifer Straub, Chelsea Smith, Tiffanie Gilbreth, Rebecca White, Tammy Schmaeng, Mamta Valderrama, Jessica Carew, Jennifer Furber, Ritu Thomas, Denise Hansen, Tess Christensen, Modena Henderson, Rebecca Smotherman, Beatta Kirr, Jennie Byrne, Manjusha Shankaradas, and Paola Turchi.

I'm grateful to my author community supporters from the International Coaching Federation North Texas Chapter Coaches, my University of Texas Dallas coaches, and Fortune 100 Coaches: Jane Koenecke, Dara Rossi, Cheryl Close, Elisabetta Mroski, Kelly O'Neil, Dr. Debra Atkisson, Rory Brannum, Vicky Hepler, Minette Velez, Lisa Ong, Marguerite Thibodeaux, Jennifer Todling, Shallyn Williams, Miao Wang, Veronica Jackson-Ratliff, Vivi Gordon, Adam Wright, Joe Lofshult, and Austin Keeton.

I appreciate the support of my author community from my family, friends, Mayo Colleagues, and past colleagues: Dr. Maile Richert, Dr. Amine Issa, Dr. Elizabeth Baden, Dr. Lilach Lerman, Dr. Karen Giles, Dr. Nick Depauw, Lynn Rekhlis, Schari Russell, Sara Oberrecht, Billie Brush, Natalie Rose, Kate Lessey, Dr. Raja Muthupillai, Fr. Thomas Behrend, Tom Flanagan, Dr. Afua Yorke, Amy Gilchrist, Misty Brownd, Harry Smith, Eric Koester, Heloiza Carman, Yolanda Vega, Dr. Tom Cull, Jayne Ragon, Miriam Pacanowski, Ed Brunins, Emily Jenkins, Barbara Gardenhire-Mills, Linsey Walker, Elfareato Remekie, Jen Shen, and Elvira Serrano.

Writing a book comes with tradeoffs. While finishing the book revisions, I was serving for a nonprofit as the communications director for the ICF North Texas Chapter. I had the presence of mind to recruit an associate director a few months after starting my term. Schartryce Mason stepped in as the associate communications director and led in my place when I had to switch lanes to support the book. She addressed the communication needs of the chapter, and she kept checking in with me along my book journey. When I speak of getting help, I speak from deep experience. Recruiting help can make you a better leader and helps you develop other leaders.

The other help I treasure are my assistants: Lesley Reinert, my executive assistant, and Savanna Phillips, my marketing assistant.

I'm deeply grateful to my choir family, my soprano sisters, our director, Ms. Freda Breed's broader vision for us, and her unwillingness to accept anything less than outstanding from us. I'm grateful to have learned so much about music from our director and our mischievous organist, Mr. Todd Hughes, whose irreverently pious humor keeps us on our toes and entertains us with his talented interludes. You know the music is good when Catholics stay after the service to hear the organists' postludes.

To my NDP family, thank you for the opportunity to publish my book. Thank you to Eric Koester and New Degree Press, to my editors, the author community, Kyra Ann Dawkins, Reilly Vore, and the entire copy editing, marketing, and graphics teams.

The book has many gymnastics references. My son decided at an early age that he wanted to be on an NCAA gymnastics team. We made several sacrifices over the years to keep him in gymnastics, including many hours spent at his gyms over the years during his training time, working on my thesis or my work projects during his training sessions, and learning the gymnastics process. He hit his target and was on the men's gymnastics team at Oklahoma University, giving me more experience in gymnastics at the elite level and enabling me to share gymnastics stories with you.

Thank you for reading *Power, Poise, and Presence*. I hope the stories and ideas in this book have inspired you to try a few new things to be powerfully, poised, and present.

Appendix

——

CHAPTER 1

Amacher, Simon Adrian, Cleo Schumacher, Corinne Legeret, Franziska Tschan, Norbert Karl Semmer, Stephan Marsch, and Sabina Hunziker. 2017. "Influence of Gender on the Performance of Cardiopulmonary Rescue Teams." *Critical Care Medicine* 45, no. 7 (July): 1184–91.

Burns, Tiffany, Jess Huang, Alexis Krivkovich, Lareina Yee, Ishanaa Rambachan, and Tijana Trkulja. 2021. "Women in the Workplace | McKinsey." McKinsey and Company. September 27, 2021. https://www.mckinsey.com/featured-insights/diversity-and-inclusion/women-in-the-workplace.

Caceres-Rodriguez, R. (2013). "The Glass Ceiling Revisited: Moving Beyond Discrimination in the Study of Gender in Public Organizations." *Administration & Society,* 45(6), (December): 674–709.

Connley, Courtney. 2021. "A Record 41 Women Are Fortune 500 CEOs—and for the First Time Two Black Women Made the

List." *CNBC.* June 2, 2021. https://www.cnbc.com/2021/06/02/
fortune-500-now-has-a-record-41-women-running-companies.
html (accessed September 9, 2022).

Dayal, Arjus, Daniel M. O'Connor, Qadri Usama, and Vineet M.
Arora. 2016. "Evaluations by Faculty During Emergency Medicine Residency Training." *JAMA Internal Medicine,* 177(5), 651.

Exley, Christine L, and Judd B Kessler. 2022. "The Gender Gap in
Self-Promotion." *The Quarterly Journal of Economics* 137, no.
3 (January): 1345–81.

Guptill, Mindi, Ellen T. Reibling, and Kathleen Clem. 2018. "Deciding to Lead: A Qualitative Study of Women Leaders in Emergency Medicine." *International Journal of Emergency Medicine*
11, no. 1 (November): 1–10. https://doi.org/10.1186/s12245-018-
0206-7.

Hewitt, Sylvia A. 2014. *Executive Presence: The Missing Link
Between Merit and Success* New York: Harper Business.

James-McCarthy, Kizanne, Andrew Brooks-McCarthy, and
Dawn-Marie Walker. 2020. "Stemming the 'Leaky Pipeline':
An Investigation of the Relationship between Work-Family
Conflict and Women's Career Progression in Academic Med-
icine." *BMJ Leader* 6, no. 2 (September 28, 2021): 110–17.

Johns Hopkins Medicine. 2021. "Risk Factors for Heart Disease:
Don't Underestimate Stress." *Health* (blog), *Johns Hopkins
Medicine.* November 3, 2021. https://www.hopkinsmedicine.
org/health/wellness-and-prevention/risk-factors-for-heart-
disease-dont-underestimate-stress.

L., Darina. 2022. "Shocking Male vs. Female CEO Statistics 2022." *Leftronic* (blog), Leftronic March 6, 2020. https://leftronic.com/blog/ceo-statistics/.

LeanIn.Org and McKinsey & Company. 2022. "Women in the Workplace 2022: The Full Report." *Women in the Workplace* (blog), Women in the Workplace. McKinsey and Company. October 18, 2022. https://www.mckinsey.com/featured-insights/diversity-and-inclusion/women-in-the-workplace.

Lim, Wee Ling, and Roziah Mohd Rasdi. 2019. "'Opt-out' or Pushed Out?" *European Journal of Training and Development* 43, no. 9 (November): 785–800.

Mahan, Thomas, Danny Nelms, Jeeun Yi, Alexander T Jackson, Michael Hein, and Richard Moffett. 2020. "Annual Employee Retention Reports | Work Institute." Work Institute, (May): 1-40. https://workinstitute.com/retention-report/.

Moss-Racusin, Corinne A., and Laurie A. Rudman. 2010. "Disruptions in Women's Self-Promotion: The Backlash Avoidance Model." *Psychology of Women Quarterly* 34, no. 2 (June): 186–202.

Nordell, Jessica. 2021. *The End of Bias: A Beginning: The Science and Practice of Overcoming Unconscious Bias.* New York: Henry Holt and Company.

OECD. 2017. *The Pursuit of Gender Equality: An Uphill Battle.* Paris, France: OECD Publishing.

Paul, Annie Murphy. 2021. *The Extended Mind: The Power of Thinking Outside the Brain*. New York: Houghton Mifflin Harcourt.

Reis, Harry T, and Susan Sprecher. 2009. *Emotional Contagion*. California: SAGE Publications.

Rudman, Laurie A. 1998. "Self-Promotion as a Risk Factor for Women: The Costs and Benefits of Counterstereotypical Impression Management." *Journal of Personality and Social Psychology* 74, no. 3 (1998): 629–45.

Salem, Victoria, Dhruti Hirani, Clare Lloyd, Lesley Regan, and Christopher J Peters. 2021. "Why Are Women Still Leaving Academic Medicine? A Qualitative Study within a London Medical School." *BMJ Open* 12, no. 6 (June). https://doi.org/10.1136/bmjopen-2021-057847.

Shook, Ellyn, and Julie Sweet. 2019. *Accenture Equality Equals Innovation Gender Equality Research Report IWD-2019*. New York: Accenture. PDF.

Vaccarino, Viola, Zakaria Almuwaqqat, Jeong Hwan Kim, Muhammad Hammadah, Amit J. Shah, Yi-An Ko, Lisa Elon, Samaah Sullivan, Anish Shah, and Ayman Alkhoder, et al. 2021. "Association of Mental Stress–Induced Myocardial Ischemia with Cardiovascular Events in Patients With Coronary Heart Disease." *JAMA* 326, no. 18 (November): 1818-1828.

Vanderkam, Laura. 2017. *I Know How She Does It: How Successful Women Make the Most of Their Time*. New York: Penguin.

Viveros Añorve, José, Jae-Hee Chang, and Linda Wirth. 2019. *Women in Business and Management: The Business Case for Change*. Geneva: International Labour Organization. PDF.

Wang, Wendy, Kim Parker, and Paul Taylor. 2013. "Breadwinner Moms | Pew Research Center." Pew Research Center. https://www.pewresearch.org/social-trends/2013/05/29/breadwinner-moms/.

CHAPTER 2

NIH. n.d. "Biomarkers." National Institute of Environmental Health Sciences. Accessed March 23, 2021. https://www.niehs.nih.gov/health/topics/science/biomarkers/index.cfm.

Paul, Annie Murphy. 2021. *The Extended Mind: The Power of Thinking Outside the Brain*. New York: Houghton Mifflin Harcourt.

United States Food and Drug Administration. 2021. "About Biomarkers and Qualification." US Food and Drug Administration. Accessed September 29, 2022. https://www.fda.gov/drugs/biomarker-qualification-program/about-biomarkers-and-qualification.

CHAPTER 3

Salimu, Y. A. 2020. *Underprivileged Overachiever: A Crenshaw Story*. Ohio: Telemachus Press.

CHAPTER 4

Aurandt, Paul, Paul Harvey, and Paul Harvey, Jr. 1978. *Paul Harvey's the Rest of the Story*. New York: Bantam.

Blake, Amanda. 2019. *Your Body Is Your Brain: Leverage Your Somatic Intelligence to Find Purpose, Build Resilience, Deepen Relationships and Lead More Powerfully.* California: Trokay Press.

Boyatzis, Richard, Melvin L. Smith, and Ellen Van Oosten. 2019. *Helping People Change: Coaching with Compassion for Lifelong Learning and Growth.* Massachusetts: Harvard Business Press.

Canpolat, Murat, Sekvan Kuzu, Bilal Yıldırım, and Sevilay Canpolat. 2015. "Active Listening Strategies of Academically Successful University Students." *Eurasian Journal of Educational Research* 15, no. 60 (September): 163–80.

Durham Peters, John. 2008. *Communication: History of the Idea.* In The International Encyclopedia of Communication, W. Donsback Ed. Chichester, UK: John Wiley & Sons, Ltd. http://dx.doi.org/10.1002/9781405186407.wbiecc075.

Fogg, BJ. 2019. *Tiny Habits: The Small Changes That Change Everything.* New York: HarperCollins.

Halonen, Risto, Liisa Kuula, Minea Antila, and Anu-Katriina Pesonen. 2021. "The Overnight Retention of Novel Metaphors Associates with Slow Oscillation–Spindle Coupling but Not with Respiratory Phase at Encoding." *Frontiers in Behavioral Neuroscience* 15 (August): 1–14.

Haney, William V. 1979. *Communication and Interpersonal Relations.* Illinois: Irwin Professional Publishing.

Hostetter, A. B., and M. W. Alibali. 2008. "Visible Embodiment: Gestures as Simulated Action." *Psychonomic Bulletin & Review* 15, no. 3 (June): 495–514.

Huseman, Richard C., James M. Lahiff, and John M. Penrose. 1991. *Business Communication: Strategies and Skills.* Chicago: Dryden Press.

Kahneman, Daniel. 2011. *Thinking, Fast and Slow.* New York: Farrar, Straus, and Giroux.

Lai, Vicky T., Olivia Howerton, and Rutvik H. Desai. 2019. "Concrete Processing of Action Metaphors: Evidence from ERP." *Brain Research* 1714 (July): 202–9.

Lotze, Martin, Katharina Erhard, Nicola Neumann, Simon B. Eickhoff, and Robert Langner. 2014. "Neural Correlates of Verbal Creativity: Differences in Resting-State Functional Connectivity Associated with Expertise in Creative Writing." *Frontiers in Human Neuroscience* 8 (July): 1–8. https://doi.org/10.3389/fnhum.2014.00516.

Marangon, Mattia, Agnieszka Kubiak, and Gregory Króliczak. 2016. "Haptically Guided Grasping. FMRI Shows Right-Hemisphere Parietal Stimulus Encoding, and Bilateral Dorso-Ventral Parietal Gradients of Object- and Action-Related Processing during Grasp Execution." *Frontiers in Human Neuroscience* 9, no. 691 (January): 1–19. https://doi.org/10.3389/fnhum.2015.00691.

Mayo Clinic Staff. 2021. "Chronic Stress Puts Your Health at Risk." *Healthy Lifestyle* (blog), Mayo Clinic. July 8, 2021. https://www.

mayoclinic.org/healthy-lifestyle/stress-management/in-depth/
stress/art-20046037.

McGann, John P. 2017. "Poor Human Olfaction Is a 19th-Century Myth." *Science* 356, no. 6338 (May): eaam7263. https://doi.org/10.1126/science.aam7263.

Mills, Fergil, Thomas E. Bartlett, Lasse Dissing-Olesen, Marta B. Wisniewska, Jacek Kuznicki, Brian A. Macvicar, Yu Tian Wang, and Shernaz X. Bamji. 2014. "Cognitive Flexibility and Long-Term Depression (LTD) Are Impaired Following β-Catenin Stabilization in Vivo." *Proceedings of the National Academy of Sciences* 111, no. 23 (May): 8631–36.

Özyürek, Aslı. 2013. "Hearing and seeing meaning in speech and gesture: insights from brain and behaviour." *Philosophical Transactions of the Royal Society B: Biological Sciences* 369, no. 1651 (September): 1–10. https://doi.org/10.1098/rstb.2013.0296.

Paul, Annie Murphy. 2021. *The Extended Mind: The Power of Thinking Outside the Brain*. New York: Houghton Mifflin Harcourt.

Ramadhani, Emilia, Dewi Kurniawati, and Dayana Dayana. 2020. "Barries to Effective Listening of Company Leaders in Medan City." *Randwick International of Social Science Journal* 1, no. 2 (August): 143–50.

Shah, Carolin, Katharina Erhard, Hanns-Josef Ortheil, Evangelia Kaza, Christof Kessler, and Martin Lotze. 2011. "Neural Correlates of Creative Writing: An FMRI Study." *Human Brain Mapping* 34, no. 5 (December): 1088–1101.

Todd, Charles. 2011. *A Test of Wills: The First Inspector Ian Rutledge Mystery*. New York: Harper Collins.

Umejima, Keita, Takuya Ibaraki, Takahiro Yamazaki, and Kuniyoshi L. Sakai. 2021. "Paper Notebooks vs. Mobile Devices: Brain Activation Differences During Memory Retrieval." *Frontiers in Behavioral Neuroscience* 15 (March): 1–11. https://doi.org/10.3389/fnbeh.2021.634158.

CHAPTER 5

Brown, Brené. 2018. *Dare to Lead: Brave Work. Tough Conversations. Whole Hearts.* New York: Random House.

Cummings, Thomas G., and Christopher G. Worley. 2014. *Organization Development and Change*. Ohio: Cengage Learning.

Franks, Steve, director. 2009. Psych. USA Network. 00:43:00.

Heuss, John. 1955. *Our Christian Vocation*. New York: Seabury Press.

Schrödinger, E. 1935. "Die Gegenwärtige Situation in Der Quantenmechanik." *Die Naturwissenschaften* 23, no. 50 (December): 844–49.

Shook, Ellyn, and Julie Sweet. 2019. *Accenture Equality Equals Innovation Gender Equality Research Report IWD-2019*. New York: Accenture. PDF.

CHAPTER 7

Boyatzis, Richard, Melvin L. Smith, and Ellen Van Oosten. 2019. *Helping People Change: Coaching with Compassion for Lifelong Learning and Growth*. Massachusetts: Harvard Business Press.

Chief. 2019. "Women have always been powerful." Chief. September 22, 2022. https://chief.com/.

Clutterbuck, David, Judie Gannon, Sandra Hayes, Ioanna Iordanou, Krister Lowe, and Doug MacKie. 2019. *The Practitioner's Handbook of Team Coaching*. Oxfordshire: Routledge.

Frankl, Viktor E. 1985. *Man's Search For Meaning*. Simon and Schuster.

Frie, Roger. 2008. *Psychological Agency*. Massachusetts: The MIT Press.

International Coaching Federation. n.d. "The Gold Standard in Coaching," Coaching Federation, August 2, 2022. https://coachingfederation.org/credentials-and-standards.

Johansson, Frans. 2017. *The Medici Effect: What Elephants and Epidemics Can Teach Us about Innovation*. Massachusetts: Harvard Business School Press.

Meijen, Carla. 2019. *Endurance Performance in Sport: Psychological Theory and Interventions*. Oxfordshire: Routledge.

Sonnenfeldt, Michael. n.d. "Home." TIGER 21, January 10, 2020. https://tiger21.com/.

Sprundel, Mariska van. 2021. *Running Smart: How Science Can Improve Your Endurance and Performance*. Massachusetts: MIT Press.

Stahl, Ashley. 2021. "This New Year's Set Goals, Not Resolutions." *Forbes*. December 9, 2021. https://www.forbes.com/sites/ashleystahl/2021/12/09/this-new-years-set-goals-not-resolutions/?sh=25bc3cc91ece (accessed August 11, 2022).

Wakefield, Simon, Paul Lee, and Matthew Guest. 2013. "Digital Collaboration: Delivering Innovation, Productivity, And Happiness." *Deloitte Digital Collaboration* (n.d): 1–24.

Walker, Matthew. 2017. *Why We Sleep: Unlocking the Power of Sleep and Dreams*. New York: Simon and Schuster.

CHAPTER 8

Basow, Susan A., Julie E. Phelan, and Laura Capotosto. 2006. "Gender Patterns in College Students' Choices of Their Best and Worst Professors." *Psychology of Women Quarterly* 30, no. 1 (March): 25–35.

Boring, Anne, Kellie Ottoboni, and Philip Stark. 2016. "Student Evaluations of Teaching (Mostly) Do Not Measure Teaching Effectiveness." *Science Open Research* 0, no. 1–11 (January): 1–11. https://doi.org/10.14293/s2199-1006.1.sor-edu.aetbzc.v1.

Clear, James. 2018. *Atomic Habits: An Easy & Proven Way to Build Good Habits & Break Bad Ones*. New York: Penguin.

Fogg, BJ. 2019. *Tiny Habits: The Small Changes That Change Everything*. New York: HarperCollins.

Hoorens, Vera, Gijs Dekkers, and Eliane Deschrijver. 2020. "Gender Bias in Student Evaluations of Teaching: Students' Self-Affirmation Reduces the Bias by Lowering Evaluations of Male Professors." *Sex Roles* 84, no. 1–2 (April): 34–48.

MacNell, Lillian, Adam Driscoll, and Andrea N. Hunt. 2014. "What's in a Name: Exposing Gender Bias in Student Ratings of Teaching." *Innovative Higher Education* 40, no. 4 (December): 291–303.

McCarthy, Colm. 2014. "Sherlock." Hartswood Films, January 26, 2014.

CHAPTER 9
Blake, Amanda. 2019. *Your Body Is Your Brain: Leverage Your Somatic Intelligence to Find Purpose, Build Resilience, Deepen Relationships and Lead More Powerfully*. California: Trokay Press.

CHAPTER 10
Boron, Walter, and Emile L. Boulpaep. 2005. *Medical Physiology: A Cellular and Molecular Approach*. Amsterdam: Elsevier.

CHAPTER 11
Grant, Adam. 2021. *Think Again: The Power of Knowing What You Don't Know*. Washington, DC: National Geographic Books.

CHAPTER 12

Fogg, BJ. 2019. *Tiny Habits: The Small Changes That Change Everything.* New York: Harper Collins.

Leone, Carmela, Peter Feys, Lousin Moumdjian, Emanuele D'Amico, Mario Zappia, and Francesco Patti. 2017. "Cognitive-Motor Dual-Task Interference: A Systematic Review of Neural Correlates." *Neuroscience & Biobehavioral Reviews* 75 (April): 348–60.

Stone, Linda. 2014. "Are You Breathing? Do You Have Email Apnea?" *Linda Stone* (blog). November 25, 2014. https://lindastone.net/2014/11/24/are-you-breathing-do-you-have-email-apnea/.

CHAPTER 13

Barnes, Jim. 2021. "Women Make up a Tiny Part of the Competitive Poker World. Here's Why." *Las Vegas Review-Journal.* July 2, 2021. https://www.reviewjournal.com/sports/poker/women-make-up-a-tiny-part-of-the-competitive-poker-world-heres-why-2391898/ (accessed September 2, 2022).

Caliendo, Frank. n.d. "Official Website of Frank Caliendo: Comedian, Actor, Impressionist." Frank Caliendo, October 26, 2018. https://www.frankcaliendo.com/.

Rowling, J.K. 2015. *Harry Potter and the Half-Blood Prince.* London: Pottermore Publishing.

Sofen, Jon. 2022. "The Muck: Why Don't More Women Play Poker?" *Poker News.* May 8, 2022. https://www.pokernews.com/

news/2022/05/women-poker-the-muck-41147.htm (accessed August 2, 2022).

CHAPTER 14

Burns, Tiffany, Jess Huang, Alexis Krivkovich, Lareina Yee, Ishanaa Rambachan, and Tijana Trkulja. 2021. "Women in the Workplace 2021." Women in the Workplace 2021. McKinsey and Company. September 27, 2021. https://www.mckinsey.com/featured-insights/diversity-and-inclusion/women-in-the-workplace.

Doldor, Elena, Madeleine Wyatt, and Jo Silvester. 2019. "Statesmen or cheerleaders? Using topic modeling to examine gendered messages in narrative developmental feedback for leaders." *The Leadership Quarterly* 30, no. 5 (October). https://doi.org/10.1016/j.leaqua.2019.101308.

Fluchtmann, Jonas, Anita Glenny, Nikolaj Arpe Harmon, and Jonas Maibom. 2022. "The Gender Application Gap: Do Men and Women Apply for the Same Jobs?" IZA Discussion Paper No. 14906 (May): 1–103.

Luft, Joseph, and Harry Ingham. 1961. "The Johari Window." *Human Relations Training News* 5, no. 1 (Summer): 6–7.

CHAPTER 15

Boyatzis, Richard, Melvin L. Smith, and Ellen Van Oosten. 2019. *Helping People Change: Coaching with Compassion for Lifelong Learning and Growth*. Massachusetts: Harvard Business Press.

Sanderson, Jim. 1982. "Liberated Male: G. W. Carver Knew Value of Sympathy." *The Sunday Pantagraph (The Pantagraph)*. October 3, 1982.

ABOUT THE AUTHOR

Lizette Warner, PhD is the Director of MR Oncology Collaborations for Philips, speaker, writer, and executive coach who turned her hand to writing after discovering a passion for helping struggling professionals through career crisis and renewal. Lizette shows her clients how to embrace "Perfect poise isn't perfect," helping professionals go be brilliant.

Lizette lives in the Dallas-Fort Worth area with her husband, a spastic Irish Wolfhound, narcoleptic Mastweiler and welcomes her nomadic children back home in between their ventures. You'll find her swimming with her team or screeching in her church choir when she isn't advising, coaching, speaking, writing, or reading. *Power, Poise, and Presence: A New Approach to Authentic Leadership* is her debut nonfiction book and her mission.

Made in the USA
Middletown, DE
19 February 2023

25179804R10166